She offers transferable actions that any couple can replicate to experience marital fulfillment."

— KERRY SHOOK, founding pastor of Woodlands
Church, Houston, Texas, and co-author of the
bestseller *One Month to Live*

"Shaunti is one of those rare communicators who really gets marriage and all the give-and-take that's required. You're holding months' worth of marital counseling in your hands!"

— SHANNON ETHRIDGE, best-selling author
of the Every Woman's Battle series

"The entire time I was reading this book I kept stopping and saying to my wife, 'Oh, wow! Listen to this!' The great truth within these pages is that little things do indeed mean a lot."

— JEFF AND GREGG FOXWORTHY

"Shaunti is one of the best researchers in the field today, and I'm always encouraged and surprised by her findings and how practical they are. I will be recommending this book to the women I minister to."

— JENNIFER ROTHSCHILD, author of *Lessons
I Learned in the Dark*

"What an important and desperately needed book! Shaunti debunks so many of the marriage myths that we have taken as gospel and shares the real secrets to happily ever after."

— KATHI LIPP, author of *The Husband Project*
and *Praying God's Word for Your Husband*

"Shaunti has done the research, dissected the results, and delivered to us the proven recipes for success. Even after thirty years of marriage, I learned so much! This is a book every married person should read!"

—JILL SAVAGE, CEO of Hearts at Home
and author of *No More Perfect Moms*

"Every married person and every person who wants to be married needs to read this book. It's a fun and surprising journey that can totally transform your marriage—I promise."

—VALORIE BURTON, author of *Happy Women Live Better*

"This book takes the mystery out of happy marriages by boiling it down to some key attitudes and actions that can make all the difference between a mediocre marriage and a magnificent one."

—LESLIE VERNICK, licensed counselor, relationship
coach, speaker, and best-selling author of
The Emotionally Destructive Marriage

"The message is timely, the research is fascinating, and the takeaways are life-impacting. Do your marriage a favor and read this book!"

—CRYSTAL PAINE, founder of MoneySavingMom.com
and author of *Say Goodbye to Survival Mode*

"This is one of the most encouraging and motivating marriage books I have ever read."

—JIM BURNS, president of HomeWord and author
of *Creating an Intimate Marriage* and *Closer*

"After working my way through these pages and pondering these gems of wisdom, I couldn't help but wonder how many marriages might have been saved had they understood these simple, attainable truths."

—SUSIE LARSON, national radio host, speaker, and author of *Your Beautiful Purpose*

"When you take the time to tune into the little things in each other, then together you'll succeed at a great marriage!"

—DR. GARY AND BARBARA ROSBERG, America's Family Coaches and authors of *6 Secrets to a Lasting Love*

"Shaunti wields the researcher's clipboard, the analyst's data, and the counselor's insight to bring the excellent newsflash that great marriages are the culmination of definable, repetitive micro-movements that add up to deep relationship satisfaction."

—ANITA RENFROE, comedian and author

"Shaunti knows how to mine scientific research and data for the relationship gold that can change marriages and change lives."

—SUSAN MERRILL, author of *The Passionate Mom,* blogger, and director of iMOM.com

—MARK MERRILL, author of *All Pro Dad,* blogger, and president of Family First

shaunti feldhahn

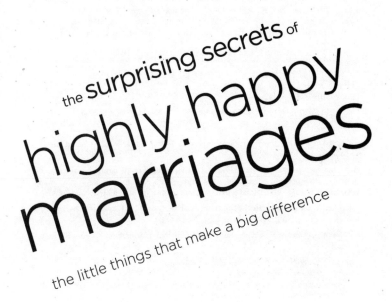

the surprising secrets of
highly happy
marriages

the little things that make a big difference

MULTNOMAH
BOOKS

THE SURPRISING SECRETS OF HIGHLY HAPPY MARRIAGES

Scripture quotations are taken from the following versions: The New American Standard Bible®. © Copyright The Lockman Foundation 1960, 1962, 1963, 1968, 1971, 1972, 1973, 1975, 1977, 1995. Used by permission. (www.Lockman.org). The Holy Bible, New International Version®, NIV®. Copyright © 1973, 1978, 1984 by Biblica Inc.™ Used by permission of Zondervan. All rights reserved worldwide. www.zondervan.com. The New King James Version®. Copyright © 1982 by Thomas Nelson Inc. Used by permission. All rights reserved. The Holy Bible, New Living Translation, copyright © 1996 and © 2007. Used by permission of Tyndale House Publishers Inc., Carol Stream, Illinois 60188. All rights reserved.

Details in some anecdotes and stories have been changed to protect the identities of the persons involved.

Hardcover ISBN 978-1-60142-121-0
eBook ISBN 978-1-60142-360-3

Copyright © 2013 by Veritas Enterprises Inc.

Cover design by Lucy Iloenyosi

Published in association with the literary agency of Calvin Edwards, 1220 Austin Glen Drive, Atlanta, Georgia 30338.

Published in the United States by Multnomah, an imprint of the Crown Publishing Group, a division of Penguin Random House LLC, New York.

MULTNOMAH® and its mountain colophon are registered trademarks of Penguin Random House LLC.

Library of Congress Cataloging-in-Publication Data
Feldhahn, Shaunti Christine.
   The surprising secrets of highly happy marriages : the little things that make a big difference / Shaunti Feldhahn. — First Edition.
      pages cm
   Includes bibliographical references.
   ISBN 978-1-60142-121-0 — ISBN 978-1-60142-360-3 (electronic) 1. Marriage.
2. Man-woman relationships. 3. Happiness. I. Title.
   HQ503.F45 2013
   306.81—dc23

                                                          2013037194

Printed in the United States of America

10

SPECIAL SALES
Most Multnomah books are available at special quantity discounts when purchased in bulk by corporations, organizations, and special-interest groups. Custom imprinting or excerpting can also be done to fit special needs. For information, please e-mail specialmarketscms@penguinrandomhouse.com or call 1-800-603-7051.

For Jeff:
My beloved, my friend…and my secret
weapon in every research project.
This book is as much yours as it is mine.

And for our children:
May you know the joy of a Yes! marriage in
His time.

Contents

The Truth About Highly Happy and You

How a Handful of High-Leverage Secrets Unlocks Delight in Your Marriage

The very first e-mail I received after the release of *For Women Only* came from an anonymous woman. I'll never forget her note. It was just one line:

I got a divorce five years ago, and now I know why.

I read it and gasped. I knew the book revealed some surprising insights about men that most women just didn't get. I had been continuously shocked myself during my years of research!

But her e-mail brought home the importance of this knowledge in a whole new way.

That was nearly ten years ago. Since then, my husband, Jeff, and I have researched and written *For Men Only* and other books. We have spoken at hundreds of conferences, seminars, churches, simulcasts, and stadium events. And during that time, literally thousands of men and women have come up to us at the book table or stopped us in a hallway. With a stunned look in their eyes, they say things like "I wish I had known this before I got married!" or "This book saved our marriage" or even "I'm going to cancel the divorce filing on Wednesday."

I'm not making this up.

Trust me, they're not talking about any special wisdom that Jeff or I have conjured up. They're talking about a before-and-after experience. What they mean is "I used to be clueless about what my spouse needed, and I didn't realize it." What they mean is "Knowing now what I totally missed before—about my spouse's inner fears and needs and desires—changes everything."

And they are right.

I started calling these breakthroughs of sudden insight "light bulb on!" moments. They land in your relationship like a bright orange marker. Before, you thought and acted one way. After, you think and act differently. You suddenly see what you didn't before. How you do a relationship—how you feel about it, what you expect, and what you get from it—changes. Light bulb on!

This book on highly happy marriages is packed with moments like that.

Without a doubt, the dream of a happy marriage is one of the most consistent longings of the human heart. Most of us deeply want to experience an abundant, delightful, lifelong companionship that we can thank God for every day. Forget the bleak statistics we've seen, forget the bad rap that committed, lifelong marriage gets in the media—we want to marry our best friend, then *enjoy* our spouse and *enjoy* being married. And many people do!

But I've also noticed that many others feel stuck in a rut and don't know how to get out of it. Some not-yet-married couples aren't sure they can navigate the transition to a lifetime commitment—or whether the dream of a forever marriage is even realistic. And many married couples—especially in times of heartache—harbor secret doubts about whether a great marriage is possible for them. Some have stopped hoping for better.

Instead of highly happy, they've settled for sometimes happy or even mostly mediocre.

But it doesn't have to be that way. You'd be surprised what a few sudden flashes of insight can do for a couple. Let me show you what I mean.

Why Do Some Marriages Turn...Good?

You may have noticed that many marriage books and efforts at relationship improvement try to increase a couple's happiness by digging into key relationship problems. Essentially, they're asking things like, "What's the underlying reason for this particular problem?" Or, bigger picture: "Why do marriages turn bad?" Identify the reason, identify the problem—and fix it. Indeed, this is great because all of us need that sort of help sometimes.

For this book, though, I aimed my research in a different direction. I wanted to know: *Why do marriages turn good?*

If a so-so union became delightful, I wanted to know what made the difference. Millions of couples truly enjoy each other in strong, rewarding relationships. What do they do right, and what can we learn from them that would make our relationships just as strong and rewarding?

It makes a lot of sense to study the winners. Aspiring athletes who want to improve how they throw a ball, swing a racket, or twist gracefully in the air to land at just the right angle on the ice spend hours studying those who do it best. Psychologists, change-management experts, and counselors have consistently found that in any endeavor of life, if we want to change, improve, or be inspired, we have to study what some call the bright spots, not just the problems. After all, if you want to be more like Jesus, you don't spend the bulk of your time studying the Pharisees, His religious-leader opponents, in order to figure out how to *not* be like them. You study Jesus.

> If we want to change, improve, or be inspired, we have to study the bright spots, not just the problems.

So for the last few years, I've been studying the bright spots in exceptionally happy marriages. Regardless of the age, cultural background, or economic situation of these lovebirds, I went looking for the answer to one overarching question:

What simple, learnable habits are common to highly happy couples—habits that they may not even realize are making them so happy, and that others can replicate?

In other words, what are the surprising secrets of highly happy marriages?

Of course, to have any hope of uncovering their secrets, we first had to identify the highly happy couples—ones who could truly inspire and educate the rest of us (whether married or not). So we went on a national search.

It happened like this.

Identifying the Yes! Couples

We started by casting a wide net. Working with more than a dozen researchers, analysts, and various specialists over the course of three years, I conducted and analyzed interviews, surveys, and focus groups with more than two thousand married men and women.[1] I gathered input from couples of different ages, ethnic groups, stages of life, cultural backgrounds, geographical areas, and religious beliefs. My interview subjects ranged from people sitting next to me on airplanes, to dozens of police officers and their spouses on a weekend getaway, to couples referred to me by counselors and community groups and readers, to hundreds of couples on a week-long marriage cruise—and many others in between. For a researcher on a mission, the world is a smorgasbord of people to hit up with questions!

Then I began to focus on what I could learn from the happiest couples. Of the roughly 1,000 couples that I interviewed and surveyed, 350 clearly revealed themselves to be bright spots, the most happily married couples whose habits I most wanted to study. To identify these role models, I asked a simple question:

> **Are you, personally, generally happy in your marriage these days and enjoying being married? (Choose one answer.)**
>
> 1. Yes!
> 2. Yes, most of the time.
> 3. It depends—sometimes yes, sometimes no.
> 4. Not really.
> 5. No! I am really unhappy.

Most answers fell into the "Yes, most of the time" category, with a bell curve on either side. For many couples, the answers were split. For example, one spouse might answer "Yes!" while the other picked "Yes, most of the time," or even one of the negative answers.

The couples I most wanted to study and learn from, however, were those where *both* the husband and the wife independently and anonymously chose "Yes!" As you will see from the survey results, there is a significant difference between a truly Yes! couple and a couple where one or both spouses answered "Yes, most of the time." You wouldn't think that there would be such a difference in how they do things in their relationship, but there is. And that difference yields gold for us as we investigate what the Yes! couples have to teach us.

First, though, we had to extract the gold. And this brings us to one of my biggest surprises about researching happy marriages:

Happy couples can rarely identify what *exactly* it is that is making them so happy! Not without some purposeful digging, that is.

> Happy couples can rarely identify what exactly it is that is making them so happy!

Maybe you've already noticed. When you ask a happy couple what they are doing that makes them so happy, they tend to smile and say something sweet and even inspiring but, honestly, not all that helpful. "Communication is absolutely vital," they'll say. Or "We learned how to fight fair." Or "We just love being with each other."

Sure, but what can you do with those comments? "Communication" or knowing how to "fight fair" sounds great but...what does that *mean*? What are they doing differently from what you are trying to do? More to the point, what is it, specifically, that *you* can do differently if you want to get their results?

In those conversations, you often walk away wishing you were more like them but not any more clear on how to get there.

A huge part of our challenge as researchers, then, was to ask the specific questions—and the telling follow-up questions—that would pull into the spotlight their hidden habits of success.

Most of the time, those critical differentiating habits were nearly invisible to the happy couple because they were actually quite...small.

> Most of the time, those critical differentiating habits were nearly invisible to the happy couple because they were actually quite...small.

It's true. In our happiness research, Jeff and I discovered again and again that contrary to popular belief, it's usually not the biggies—in-laws, money, sex—that determine the level of day-to-day mutual happiness in a marriage. Much more often, it's daily unspoken beliefs, assumptions, and practices that make the difference *regardless* of the big issues. In other words, it is *how* we handle those issues that determines how much we enjoy marriage.

Small difference makers, maybe. But immensely powerful, and—for you and me—nearly priceless. Because once you know that they make a difference, you can do them on purpose. And even though most of us overlook them, they tend to be as close as the end of your nose. I'll give you an example.

Priceless Discoveries Just Out of Sight

At one marriage conference Jeff and I did for dozens of first responders and their spouses, we conducted a real-time keypad survey and (as we always do) had spouses sit on opposite sides of the room so they could be completely candid in their answers about what were largely high-stress marriages. After the group came back together, we projected the answers on the screen.

The final slide, which we left up on the screen, showed the results to a question asking how they felt about their spouses. Fully 95 percent of those in the room answered that they "absolutely" cared about their spouses (just 5 percent answered "sometimes," with zero saying that they didn't really want the best for their spouses anymore). But when the respondents were asked if they *knew* their spouses wanted the best for them, only about half answered yes.

One of the conference organizers came up to us afterward and said, "What I really loved was that you left that last graph up on the screen through the rest of the talk so the good news was right in front of people, including all the hurting couples who were there. It points out that no matter how you might *feel,* this is the reality, people!"

Did you catch the powerful surprise in the data? Here it is:

(!) Nearly everyone cares about his or her spouse (100 percent of the people in that room), but only half of those spouses *actually believe it.*

That's why we left that whopping 95 percent / 5 percent / 0 percent finding up in front of that group—to reveal what so many well-intentioned spouses miss or somehow forget, especially in the heat of the moment. Because here's the happiness secret that arises from it:

(!) Highly happy spouses *choose* to believe their mate cares for them—no matter what they're seeing from their spouse or feeling at the time—and they act accordingly.

As you'll discover in just a few pages ahead, this one small choice makes a world of difference.

I found a dozen of these high-leverage secrets—little habits that bring big benefits to a marriage. Amazingly, most of these actions are truly simple. They are not always easy, mind you— some require serious self-discipline at first—but I can assure you that not even one is out of reach for the average couple. You just first have to know they matter in order to be purposeful about trying them!

Finding the Patterns,
Conducting the Surveys

Although these secrets are simple to understand, they weren't simple to uncover. Here's how we did it.

In every survey throughout our process, respondents were anonymous and the spouses never saw each other's answers so everyone could be completely candid. In every interview and focus group, participants were assured anonymity so they could be direct and honest. So very early on, patterns began to emerge and important distinctions surfaced. For example, the things that the happiest couples tended to do that helped *make them* so happy as opposed to things they did solely *because* they were happy.

To investigate those patterns further and to test whether they were indeed common and effective to creating happy couples, we did two different types of surveys, turning to a team with whom I have worked on six different books and studies. (You can see the other studies at www.shaunti.com.) Dr. Chuck Cowan, the former chief of survey design at the US Census Bureau and the founder of the highly regarded company Analytic Focus, helped me create well-designed surveys.

The first were independent surveys of 796 people (398 couples); these were paper-based, direct-response (keypad), or online surveys in many different marriage-related venues. Since many such arenas tend to be associated with churches, this group had a high percentage of churchgoers.

Then it was time for the nationally representative survey. To conduct the survey itself, as I have many times in the past, I relied on the team at Decision Analyst, one of the top companies in the world for conducting this type of reliable online survey. The survey was nationally representative across all demographic categories, assessed 508 men and women (254 married couples), and provided a confidence level of 95 percent, plus or minus 5 percent.[2] (For more details, see the methodology chapter written by Chuck Cowan at the website for this book, www.surprising secrets.com.)

Although I primarily relied on this survey, in a few cases, under Chuck's guidance, I wanted to do a type of meta-analysis and look at the results of *all* the data sets I had gathered—both the nationally representative and churchgoers' results together. I will refer to that as the combined survey.

Also, unlike in most of my past books, there is another type of research included. Several of the habits I identified in happy couples intersect with subjects that have been independently studied by other researchers, particularly Dr. Brad Wilcox of the University of Virginia and the National Marriage Project. I was grateful Dr. Wilcox and several other researchers were willing to conduct specialized runs of their survey data for inclusion in this book. You'll see those findings in four of the chapters to follow.

How to Read This Book

This book describes the simple, often-overlooked but vitally important habits that help create happy couples. To get the most out of the material, here are a few things you need to know.

1. Know What This Book Is...and Isn't

This is a bit different from most other marriage and relationship books. For one thing, it is not designed to cover everything that will help you have a good marriage. Many excellent books already go into great depth about communication skills, for example, or principles for handling conflict, or how to handle specific problem areas. But this book focuses on the little things that make a big difference *regardless* of the other challenges you might be facing—and even (in most cases) regardless of whether you're already married or simply in a serious relationship.

Keep in mind that I never intend to suggest that there is always a quick fix for marital happiness. And I don't want to make light of the many truly difficult relationship situations that couples find themselves in. Some will require professional counseling. And for some couples, the issues they are facing go far, far beyond the scope of this book.

So in an imperfect world with imperfect people, the operative words about the impact of these habits are *often* or *likely*, rather than *always* or *guaranteed*. I wish everything would turn out right when we try to do the right things, but we all know it just doesn't always happen that way. (And as you will see in chapter 11, it is so important to keep a good perspective about marital happiness, anyway.)

But these cautions notwithstanding, my research consistently shows that many marriages that have become deeply unhappy don't have to be. Not to mention that many marriages are already good and looking to be great! The key is that no matter the state of your marriage, small changes in awareness and action truly can change everything.

2. Recognize That the Research Was Rigorous Regardless of Belief System, but There Are Certain Faith-Based Applications

As some of you know, I come at life (and this book) from a Christian worldview. But, as always, the research in this book was rigorously conducted with people of all demographic and religious backgrounds, and the nationally representative survey clearly showed that the conclusions apply to everyone.

In several cases I make faith-based references where my research found the same conclusion that is discussed in the Bible, or where the application clearly parallels Judeo-Christian beliefs. I start from the assumption that given the rigor of the research, most readers will be fine with faith-based references, even if they may not personally share those beliefs.

3. Understand How to Read the Survey Responses and Compare Them to Your Own Relationship

Within each chapter, and in the more detailed Survey Says section at the end of each chapter, I present the survey results so you can not only see how the happiest couples handle things but so you can easily compare their answers to those in other types of marriages—such as, perhaps, yours.

Instead of presenting an average of all the survey responses as I have done in my other books, I slot the survey takers (and their answers) into three groups. These three groups are based on their answers to the "Are you generally happy and enjoying being married?" question:

1. **Highly happy couples**—where *both* the husband and wife, taking surveys separately, independently answered "Yes!" to that question. These are the role-model "Yes! couples" that I refer to throughout the book.

2. **Mostly happy couples**—where one spouse answered "Yes!" and the other "Yes, most of the time," or both spouses answered "Yes, most of the time."

3. **So-so or struggling couples**—where one or both spouses answered "Sometimes yes; sometimes no," "Not really," or "No!" to that question. If one partner answered that they were happy but the other partner chose one of those three "no" answers, the couple was put in the so-so or struggling category. For simplicity, we are labeling these as struggling couples, although many of these couples wouldn't think of themselves as struggling as much as simply not being as happy as they would like to be.

Each time I show a survey result in the pages that follow, I show the answers of each of these three groups.

4. Understand How to Read and Apply These Truths

The goal of this book isn't academic; it's personal. I want to show you what matters—that you didn't realize mattered!—so you see what you can do to improve your marriage *a lot*. To this end, you'll see ideas and suggestions from me or the people I interview scattered throughout the chapters. You may want to read with a pen or pencil in hand so that you can circle the insights that seem especially important to you. Make notes on how you could apply those ideas to your life. Our concluding chapter will give you some specific, practical ways to put these ideas to work, starting with giving yourself credit for what you are already doing well (very important!), picking just one or two habits that you want to start working on, and then being aware of the cool things that happen next so you are incentivized to keep trying.

This leads me to caution: Don't try to apply every new idea at the same time! Couples applying these findings have found that tackling too many at once results in getting overwhelmed enough not to do *any* of them. Pick one idea first, and try it for a week or two or five. Then when that action becomes a habit, start on another.

"But Is a Happy Marriage in the Cards for *Me*?"

Maybe you've read this far with a nagging doubt in your heart that says, *But, Shaunti, what about me? I'm not sure we're a Yes! couple or ever could be. To put it bluntly, you've never met Henry!* (Or maybe it's Henrietta.) *Are you saying a happy marriage is possible? Even for me?*

My friend, I understand your hesitation. I've heard from hundreds of sincerely motivated spouses whose hope for a happy marriage has been badly shaken. But I strongly encourage you to read on. *This book was written with exactly you in mind*—and many of the husbands and wives who poured out their hearts to me in my research had you in mind too. In fact, many of them started where you are today. That is why I'm so eager to share the hidden little habits that can change a contentious marriage into a delightful one!

It turns out that positive changes in a marriage rarely depend on one difficult spouse suddenly becoming an altogether different person. Usually, the opposite is true. Change—even in challenging marriages—most often starts with one immediate, practical, and surprising choice. A choice made by *just one* partner. And you can make it. The day you put one surprising secret to work in your relationship—and then another—may go unnoticed by your partner. But you have launched an insurrection against mediocrity and unhappiness.

Our research clearly shows that if *one* spouse commits to applying the simple but powerful habits we describe in this book—and does them sacrificially and for as long as it takes—most marriages end up being transformed. And it is because of this fact that I can assure you that a delightful, strong, happy marriage is not only *possible* but *likely*. Not guaranteed, but certainly likely. Our Yes! couples have convinced us of that.

And, thankfully, getting to highly happy is actually a lot simpler and easier than you probably realize. By the time you are done with this short book, I hope you agree with me.

> Even if just one spouse commits to applying these simple but powerful habits, most marriages end up being transformed.

So are you ready to learn the eyeopening secrets of highly happy couples and experience them in *your* marriage? Let's look at the first one together.

Know Little Is Big

Why a Few Small Actions
Carry Such Surprising Power

Not long ago, the marriage of some close friends—I'll call them Daniel and Jessica—suddenly imploded. We did everything we could to stand with them in their crisis and to speak hope for their future together. Unfortunately, their marriage didn't survive.

I'll never forget a conversation I had with Jessica one day as she grieved the loss of her marriage. Through her sobs, she said, "He worked so hard for a year to take us on that amazing vacation to Hawaii. But all I really wanted was for him to put his arm around me in church!"

Huh? Do you think in the midst of all her pain that she was thinking clearly?

Actually, I do.

I could fill in lots of other details, but ultimately the pattern is a sadly common one. You may have seen it too. Daniel was a godly, well-intentioned husband who showed his love in several ways, including working long hours to provide for his family and to do nice things for them. You see, for him, providing *is* love. Unfortunately, he didn't realize that what he was working so hard for wasn't what Jessica most needed—and in some ways was actually robbing her of the closeness she needed most. (And of course there were ways she didn't know she was hurting him.) What she needed most, more than all the expensive vacations in the world, were a few, simple, specific day-to-day actions.

But as simple as a loving gesture in public? you wonder.

Yes! My research on happy couples showed that an extraordinarily high percentage of them were (often without realizing it!) doing a few, little specific actions that were making their spouses feel deeply cared for. Jessica, as it turns out, is like nearly all other men and women in her deep-rooted desire for these surprisingly meaningful gestures.

Clearly, a few small actions won't fix deep relationship problems. But for most of us, a handful of simple day-to-day actions increase the *likelihood that our spouse feels that we care deeply about them, instead of feeling that we don't.* There's just enormous power in that!

> A handful of simple day-to-day actions increase the likelihood that our spouse feels that we care deeply about them, instead of feeling that we don't.

Identifying these little but powerful practices and showing you how to put them to work in your marriage is what this chapter is about.

The Few, the Small...the Huge

In our surveys, two categories of a few small actions surfaced. The first category consists of a few specific *things that matter to almost every member of your spouse's gender.* But they are so small you just need to notice that they matter. These same actions have the power to make almost every man or almost every woman feel loved and cared for. And happiness results.

The second category of a few small actions is not as universal. Likely, they don't even matter to a majority of people who seem to be very similar to your spouse. But they matter enormously to *your* spouse! They speak convincingly of love and care to him or her in particular, so doing these actions results in even more happiness.

When a husband or wife puts in the modest effort it takes to learn both categories of a few small actions, it is like suddenly seeing springs of water irrigating a dry plain. Happy moments begin to bloom all over the place, and enduring love puts down roots. Simply stated, here's the surprising two-part secret:

> For nearly every man or woman, the same few, small gender-specific actions not only matter but have a huge impact on a couple's level of happiness. But these little actions take on even more power when accompanied by those that matter to your spouse individually.

Maybe now you can see why I call these few small actions *huge.*

What I noticed in my research is that if most of us aren't doing these little things, it's not out of a desire to withhold them. Mostly, we just don't think about them or we don't realize just how massively important they are. They feel too simple to really matter that much. Or, in some cases, they feel awkward.

On the other hand, spouses in highly happy marriages— those Yes! couples where both husband and wife independently said they were at the highest level of happiness—consistently do these few small actions. And they get the predictable results: their spouses become happier—and usually so do they!

The Fantastic Five for Him, for Her

Let's begin with the few small actions that the surveys indicate matter a lot to almost every man or every woman—what we might call the Fantastic Five.

When individuals were asked on the surveys if a particular action made them happy, the affirmative response numbers were staggeringly high for *five specific actions* for each gender, even among the struggling couples. Close to 100 percent of all husbands and wives said these actions mattered, with between 65 and 90 percent of all husbands and wives saying these actions would deeply please them. (See Survey Says at the end of this chapter for more.)

In other words, *you are very likely to make your spouse feel deeply cared for if you make a habit of doing the same five things consistently.*

First, let's look at the five most impactful little things a wife can do to boost her husband's happiness, and then we'll switch and look at the things a husband can do to increase his wife's happiness.

The Fantastic Five for Him

A wife will have a big impact on her husband's happiness when she does the following.

1. Notices his effort and sincerely thanks him for it. (For example, she says "Thank you for mowing the lawn even though it was so hot outside" or "Thanks for playing with the kids, even when you were so tired from work.") This deeply pleases 72 percent of all men (see bar graph below).

2. Says "You did a great job at _____." This deeply pleases 69 percent of all men.

3. Mentions in front of others something he did well. This deeply pleases 72 percent of all men.

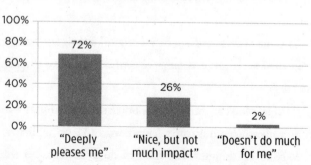

How much hearing "Thank you" matters to men

Average of all men, regardless of happiness category.

4. Shows that she desires him sexually and that he pleases her sexually. This deeply pleases 85 percent of all men.

5. Makes it clear to him that he makes her happy. (For example, she expresses appreciation for something he did for her with a smile, words, a big hug, etc.) This deeply pleases 88 percent of all men.

Now let's look at the five best little things a husband can do that usually make his wife feel greatly cared for.

The Fantastic Five for Her

On his side, a husband will have a big impact on his wife when he does the following.

1. Takes her hand. (For example, when walking through a parking lot or sitting together at the movies.) This deeply pleases 82 percent of all women (see bar graph below).

2. Leaves her a message by voice mail, e-mail, or text during the day to say he loves and is thinking about her. This deeply pleases 75 percent of all women.

3. Puts his arm around her or lays his hand on her knee when they are sitting next to each other in public (at church, at a restaurant with friends, etc.). This deeply pleases 74 percent of all women.

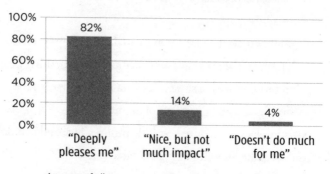

How much it matters when he reaches out and takes her hand

Average of all women, regardless of happiness category.

4. Tells her sincerely "You are beautiful." This deeply pleases 76 percent of all women.

5. Pulls himself out of a funk when he's morose, grumpy, or upset about something, instead of withdrawing. (This doesn't mean he doesn't get angry or need space; it means he tries to pull himself out of it.) This deeply pleases 72 percent of all women.

Keys That Unlock Any Door

Did you notice that *all* these happiness-inducing actions are simple, learnable, and doable by any wife or any husband? This is great news since (as you can see from the Survey Says section) the extremely high numbers for it "deeply pleases me" show how important these actions are.

Honestly, even if you read no further in this book and just put each of the five biggest little things to work every day, I'm betting your marriage will improve—in some cases, radically.

And here's more great news: All these small but powerful actions matter *regardless of what the person's love language is.*[3] For example, most wives (82 percent) are affected when her husband reaches out and takes her hand, regardless of whether physical touch is her thing.*

Case in point: Two separate women described to me why small physical gestures were so important, even though physical touch wasn't really a top love language for either of them. "If he's touching my back, it communicates things are okay," one explained. "If he's *reaching over* and touching me, it says things are good."

The other woman explained it like this: "When we are out with friends at a restaurant and he leans back and puts his arm

---

* There was one small exception worth noting: in struggling marriages, while 75 percent of wives said a husband's physical gesture to (for example) take his wife's hand would have a very positive impact, that gesture would not be appreciated among one in ten struggling couples. In interviews with wives of the latter type (the 10 percent), they said trust would need to be reestablished before that type of intimate gesture would seem appropriate.

around me, it is like he is saying 'You're mine.' I cannot tell you how special that feels."

Looking at what feels special to men, I was still shocked—even after all my years of research—to learn that my husband and most other men are so deeply touched by receiving a simple "Thank you" from their wives. In fact, most husbands (72 percent) are powerfully affected by "Thank you" even if words of affirmation is not their love language.

It finally clicked for me that because a man's greatest desire is to do something well—and have it be noticed and appreciated—*a woman's saying "Thank you" to her man is the emotional equivalent of his saying "I love you" to her.* Listen to how another husband explained the reason those words have so much power:

> A woman's saying "Thank you" to
> her man is the emotional equivalent
> of his saying "I love you" to her.

When she says "Thank you" and I know she means it, it makes me feel needed. Sometimes I feel insecure about my ability to fix stuff around the house or plan that special date night. So I may feel like I didn't do such a good job. But then if she says she actually likes what I did for her, that one thing gives me strength to keep trying. Her opinion is the one that matters the most to me. When she tells me "Thank you," no matter what else is going wrong in my world, that simple act does wonders for me.

Women tend to *think* grateful thoughts, but maybe we don't realize how important it is to *say* them! When I asked on Facebook one day what it means when "a wife notices what you did for her and says 'Thank you,'" a man echoed many others when he replied, "Everything. It means everything. It makes me feel like Superman."

A Closer Look

Now, before we move on, let's take a closer look at two of the most surprising, best little things from the Fantastic Five—one for each gender. Both are incredibly important but usually overlooked.

1. It's Not Just a Platitude: He Really Wants Her to Let Him Know That He's Made Her Happy!

I must confess it actually took me years to understand what I was hearing when so many men said, "I just want my wife to be happy." I discounted their comments since I assumed they were saying it because it's something they felt they should say.

Finally, I realized, *No! This is real!* A man is powerfully motivated to make his wife happy and powerfully impacted when his wife makes it clear that he's succeeded.

A man will feel on top of the world with something as simple as seeing a big smile on his wife's face when she comes into the kitchen and notices he's cleaned it. Conversely, seeing a little frown and watching her take out the sponge to reclean the countertops sends his stomach sinking. And this is true for 90 percent of the men on the survey!

Look at how one young husband (married seven years) described the power of knowing that he's pleased his wife in the day-to-day aspects of life:

> Knowing that I was able to please her feels so good. Life
> can be stressful, and you want to be able to do something
> to make her happy and content instead. Her big smile, or
> a hug or kiss, signals that everything else has disappeared
> and she forgets about the stress for a while. Sometimes she
> drops what she's doing and looks really pleased with me.
> Yeah, I love that.

2. It's Not a Trifle: It Is Huge for Her When He Tries to Pull Himself Out of a Bad Mood

It often surprises a man to learn that when he is in a funk, withdrawn, or a bit morose, it greatly affects his wife and (if he has them) his kids. His wife, especially, worries not just about him (*Is he okay?*) but also about the relationship (*Are we okay?*).

A few years ago I read the Harry Potter books to see what all the fuss was about. In the fifth book, *Harry Potter and the Order of the Phoenix,* I happened upon a word picture that perfectly captured what so many women described: In this story, one of the major characters is feeling lonely and isolated in his gloomy mansion, and he is thus delighted to have an unexpected, lively house full of guests over Christmas. But the story goes on,

> As the date of their departure...drew nearer, he became more and more prone to what Mrs. Weasley called "fits of the sullens," in which he would become taciturn and grumpy, often withdrawing to [a remote room] for hours at a time. His gloom seeped through the house, oozing under doorways like some noxious gas, so that all of them became infected by it.[4]

Just as these "fits of the sullens" negatively affect everyone else, a man's visible efforts to change his mood can have a hugely positive effect—especially on the woman in his life.

I can testify that one of the main reasons my own marriage is so happy is that Jeff has figured out how to pull himself out of a bad mood. Over the years, he's shortened his recovery time from several days to several hours. Sometimes he can even shake it off in minutes. I know it's not easy for him, but his actions in this one area are a tangible gift to our family. They dramatically improve my own sense of well-being and make me so much happier.

The Best Little Personal Things

In addition to the Fantastic Five little things that matter to nearly every man or woman, there are those little things that matter specifically to *your* mate. Finding out what those are are—and committing to do them—will increase your spouse's happiness (and your own) even more.

This is where a person's love language comes into the picture. But what surprised me most in my interviews was that it was not the action itself that was most important, but rather what the action implied. In other words, the *why* behind the action that says "My spouse knows what matters to me and makes sure to do it—and that means they care about me."

Whenever a husband or wife said he or she felt very cared for, I always asked, "What is it that your spouse does, specifically, that is making you feel so cared for?" Here's what one woman said about her husband's actions that communicated "I care about what matters *to you.*"

I know it sounds so simple, but he makes me a bowl of oatmeal in the morning so I can gulp it down before running off to work—he knows I wouldn't eat otherwise. And another thing: he's a late-night guy who stays up till all hours working on something, but he knows I don't want to go to bed by myself. So he comes in and lies down with me until I am asleep and then sneaks out.

Or, if I see a woman in a little outfit and say, "Oh, I like that dress; she's cute," or even "That skirt is too short," his response is always, "Who?! What?! I didn't see it!" He's a really smart guy! And to me, all those things say "I love you."

By contrast, the best little personal things that tended to matter to men were the things that made them feel appreciated. One young husband told me,

What comes to mind is that work can be a burden, and my wife is really good at expressing "Good job at that" or "Thanks for working so hard today." When I come home and she's done with work for the day and meets me at the door and gives me a hug and says "Thanks for working hard for us," I can tell that she means what she's saying and she's also excited that I've come home. It just really affirms what I'm doing and the time I've put in at work.

It is simply a really great feeling that comes when
I try to do something for her, and she has that response.
I love seeing that response.

Now, the funny thing is, I can almost guarantee that most readers are looking at what the *other* gender said throughout this chapter and are feeling vaguely disappointed because these particular "secrets" seem so...minor. The average guy may be thinking, *I mean, come on! Putting my arm around her in church is hardly profound.* Or the average woman is thinking, *Seriously? You can't mean that smiling and giving him a thank-you hug for doing the dishes is really going to matter?*

Well, yes, it is. And, yes, I can. If you don't believe me, there's an easy test: Ask the person in your life. And—assuming your spouse is in the majority—be willing to try it and watch what happens.

That is basically what Jeff and I have done over the last ten years as we have been continuously surprised by our research into what matters. As Jeff put it, "Guys sometimes feel helpless because they don't always know what's causing their wife's feelings to change for better or for worse. I might see that she's happier today, but my hypothesis is that she had a good night's sleep, not that I put my arm around her in church. But once I know that there is something specific that put her in a good mood, it is replicable. Once I know that matters, I can do it again."

There's no looking back for our friends Jessica and Daniel. But I'm so thankful that God is good. He is always at work to redeem our broken parts—and I know He'll do it for our friends. Still, a corner of my heart mourns the heartbreak that might have been prevented if they had truly understood the power of doing these best little things.

We all know that small, thoughtful acts are not a magic cure-all for every marriage problem. But having talked to so many who nurtured so much happiness with simple but powerful actions, I know all of us can build that all-important foundation that helps us believe that our mate notices and cares.

Because as it turns out, *believing that the other person cares* is far more important to building a happy marriage than most of us ever realized. Let's turn to chapter 3 and look at this next secret together.

Survey Says

Below are the survey results of three scenarios presented to the men, and three presented to the women. You can see the rest at our website, www.surprisingsecrets.com.

First are the scenarios given to a *husband* about his *wife's* actions. In each example, the husband was asked to indicate how happy or filled up it makes him when (or if) his wife did each of the things indicated. In *every category* of marriage—highly happy, mostly happy, and struggling—the outsized positive impact is noticeably large.

She notices when I do something and sincerely thanks me for it. (For example: "Thank you for mowing the lawn even though it was so hot outside" or "Thanks for playing with the kids, even when you were so tired from work.")

	Highly Happy Couples	Mostly Happy Couples	Struggling Couples
It deeply pleases me—it's a small thing that has a relatively big impact.	79%	68%	65%
It feels nice, but not much impact.	21%	32%	26%
It doesn't do much for me.	0%	0%	9%

She makes it clear that she desires me sexually (she initiates physical intimacy at times, she is not just "willing" but enthusiastic, etc.) and/or that I please her sexually.

	Highly Happy Couples	Mostly Happy Couples	Struggling Couples
It deeply pleases me—it's a small thing that has a relatively big impact.	84%	87%	86%
It feels nice, but not much impact.	14%	11%	11%
It doesn't do much for me.	2%	2%	4%

Note: Due to rounding, some percentages do not total 100%.

She makes it clear that I make her happy (appreciates something I did for her, smiles, etc.).

	Highly Happy Couples	Mostly Happy Couples	Struggling Couples
It deeply pleases me— it's a small thing that has a relatively big impact.	90%	90%	83%
It feels nice, but not much impact.	10%	10%	18%
It doesn't do much for me.	0%	0%	0%

Note: Due to rounding, some percentages do not total 100%.

Next are the survey results of three of the scenarios given to the *wife* about her *husband's* actions. In each example, the wife was asked to indicate how happy or filled up it makes her when (or if) her husband did each of the things indicated. Each of these actions mattered a lot, regardless of how happy their marriage was.

He reaches out and takes my hand. (For example, when we are walking through a parking lot or sitting together at the movies.)

	Highly Happy Couples	Mostly Happy Couples	Struggling Couples
It deeply pleases me— it's a small thing that has a relatively big impact.	90%	78%	75%
It feels nice, but not much impact.	9%	18%	16%
It doesn't do much for me.	1%	4%	9%

He leaves me a quick voice mail or text message during the day to say he's thinking about me.

	Highly Happy Couples	Mostly Happy Couples	Struggling Couples
It deeply pleases me—it's a small thing that has a relatively big impact.	76%	72%	77%
It feels nice, but not much impact.	18%	22%	18%
It doesn't do much for me.	6%	6%	5%

He pulls himself out of a "funk" when he's in a bad mood or upset about something, instead of withdrawing.

	Highly Happy Couples	Mostly Happy Couples	Struggling Couples
It deeply pleases me—it's a small thing that has a relatively big impact.	71%	75%	68%
It feels nice, but not much impact.	26%	20%	25%
It doesn't do much for me.	3%	5%	7%

Believe the Best

How Assuming That Your Spouse Cares Deeply Changes Everything

I promise the husband you're about to meet—his name is David—is a good guy who is considerate and loving toward his wife. The thing is, based on what happens in the story you're about to read, you may not believe it at first.

Sandy and David are in their early forties, have been married sixteen years, and are raising three school-age boys. Funny and sharp, both work in busy jobs. And they have just gone through an exhausting few months. David recently lost his mother to a terminal illness, and the emotional trauma, medical details, and half-day drives back and forth to support his father have left Sandy and David weary to the bone.

Finally, they saw blue sky ahead—a Saturday with no obligations, an opportunity to get their life back, rest, and just unwind. David set up a morning sports outing with his best buddies whom he hadn't seen in months. Sandy looked forward to a dinner-and-a-movie date with David later that afternoon and evening. She arranged for their kids to spend the day and night with her mom, bought a new outfit to make David's eyes pop, and planned the perfect date—all the way from drinks on their little deck as soon as he got home, to candles in the bedroom when they returned from their outing.

Saturday morning arrived, and Sandy waved as David drove away, after promising he'd be home in good time for their date. But the afternoon arrived and he didn't. About three o'clock, Sandy texted him to ask when he'd be home. He texted back that he'd had a few beers and was really tired from a day in the sun. He needed to wait a bit before driving, but he'd be home soon.

Sandy started to get nervous about time slipping away, even though they hadn't set a time for David to be back. But she knew he wanted to go out with her that evening, so she waited.

At five o'clock, David texted an apology that he still wasn't back. Stifling frustration, Sandy thought, *Well, we can skip the movie and just do dinner.*

Shortly after six o'clock, he got home. "I'll just take a quick shower and we can go," he told her. But she noticed how exhausted he looked, sighed to herself, and said, "Why don't you take a thirty-minute nap?" Relieved, he showered and fell into bed.

Another hour passed.

Sandy, whose compassion was running out like the sand in an hourglass, was now angry and hurt. She sat on their deck and poured herself one of the drinks she had planned for them to share, fuming that she'd done so many things to make this date special and that he apparently cared so little about it.

At half past eight, David came blearily downstairs, with great trepidation, to find Sandy dressed in comfy pajamas, snacking on mac and cheese, and watching an episode of *Mad Men* on Netflix. He wasn't surprised when she told him she didn't want to go out to dinner so late. He wasn't surprised that she didn't want to try to go get dessert or do something that would now not be a special date, but something forced. And he certainly wasn't surprised to hear that the candles in the bedroom would not be lit that night. But he was stunned to hear that she was no longer upset.

"You're...you're not mad?" He looked at her, shocked. "You should be."

Something had happened that replaced her anger with calmness.

"No. I'm really disappointed," she said. "Really, really disappointed. We finally had some quality time for ourselves without the kids, and we didn't get to use it because you didn't come home when you said you would. But _____.
And I know you needed this time with your friends."

Are you looking at that big blank space in her statement to her husband? "But..."

But what? What was it that changed in her mind—and in her heart? What was it that caused her to change how she felt about her husband and to respond to his legitimately hurtful action in a way that *preserved* their happiness as a couple rather than hindered it?

Here is what she said to him: "But I know you love me. And I know you needed this time with your friends."

So simple. But so important. Not "You didn't care about me" but instead *"I know you love me."*

David, overwhelmed at her gentle reaction, pulled her into a hug and said, "I'm so sorry. I'm such a bonehead. Can we try this again soon—whenever we can get a baby-sitter?"

"Yes," she affirmed.

He held her tighter. "I don't deserve you, you know."

Sandy grinned. "I know."

Assume the Best, Act on the Best

The finding of this chapter may be the most important one—a prerequisite, even—for anyone who wants a highly happy marriage. When I explored what happens when one spouse hurts or disappoints the other, I found a truly stunning difference between the happiest couples...and everyone else.

In struggling or even mostly happy marriages, hurt spouses routinely but subconsciously assumed that the offending party didn't really care about them. The unseen internal assumption was something like "He knew how that would make me feel—and he did it anyway."

In other words, although they may not have *consciously* thought about it in this way, they were assuming their spouse intended to hurt them. They were, in fact, assuming the worst of their spouse's intentions.

> The internal assumption of the highly happy spouses was "He must not have known how that would make me feel, or he wouldn't have done it."

Not so in highly happy marriages. Even when hurting spouses couldn't completely explain what had happened, they *resolutely assumed that their mates cared about them and had no intention of hurting them to begin with.* The internal assumption of these Yes! spouses was something like "He must not have known how that would make me feel, or he wouldn't have done it."

Like Sandy in our story above, the highly happy spouses still experienced the painful feelings—sometimes quite intensely. But they refused to believe the pain was intended. This made it easier to let the pain go rather than hold on to it.

In other words, they forced themselves to *not* believe the worst motivation—and to believe the best instead. To sum up our surprising secret,

> When highly happy spouses are legitimately hurt, they refuse to believe that their mate *intended* to hurt them, and they look for the most generous explanation instead.

In fact, this is almost a prerequisite for a highly happy marriage, as it is difficult to be happily married without it.

Now, if you are being regularly hurt by your spouse in some way, you may have trouble grasping why any reasonably smart person would make such a foolish, wimpy, and possibly even dangerous assumption. *What do you mean he didn't plan to hurt me? Look what he did! Look how it made me feel!*

In these circumstances, which exist even in the most fulfilling relationships, happy couples have learned to see things differently. Stay with me, because it takes not one but two survey results to see the secret.

First, all our survey results over the last ten years have confirmed that most married individuals deeply care about their spouse. Even if they don't always know how to show it, even if they are angry or upset right at that moment, and even in the most struggling marriages, they sincerely care about the person they married.

> All our survey results over the last ten years have confirmed that most married individuals deeply care about their spouse.

Among highly happy and mostly happy spouses, that fact is almost unanimous. Even among the most struggling couples, 97 percent said they cared about their mates, with eight in ten saying "Yes, absolutely." In fact, out of the 1,261 people officially surveyed, only nine people said "Not really." Not 9 percent but nine *people*!

The graph on the next page shows the combined survey results.

Do you see the overwhelming evidence that nearly all spouses

Percent who care about their spouse and want the best for them, even during painful times

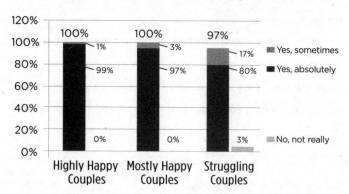

care for each other? And let's personalize this: Do you see the overwhelming evidence that *your* spouse cares about *you*? The nearly universal truth is that each spouse sincerely wants the best for the other, even during painful times.

But the story doesn't end there. As the next survey question reveals, some spouses believe that nearly universal reality, but many don't—and this is one of the main causes for the difference in their level of happiness.

Take a look at the responses given when asked "Is the following statement true or false? 'Even in the middle of a painful argument, I know that my spouse is fully "for me" and deeply cares about me.'"

Where the first question revealed the across-the-board truth

Percent who know their spouse does care about them, even during an argument

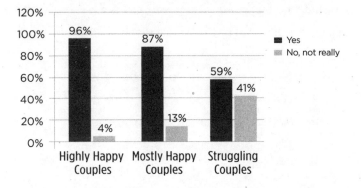

that spouses *do* care for their mates, the second question shows that there are some mostly happy and a lot of struggling spouses who don't think their mates feel the same way.

Remember, even in struggling relationships, 97 percent of spouses said they cared about their mates. But more than four in ten believe their spouses *don't* care about them.

Of course, sadly, there are some people who are truly spiteful, self-centered, and hurtful. Some marriages have deteriorated to one unkind exchange after another. Some spouses should *not* be trusted to come through. Some of us have seen these marriages; maybe some of us are even in them. But statistically, these marriages are rare. And again, what the numbers reveal is how dramatically high the proportion is of spouses who truly care.

For the vast majority of couples, if all those numbers are accurate, there is only one possible conclusion: Nearly every wife or husband who thinks *My spouse doesn't care* is flat wrong. Their unhappiness is caused by a belief that simply isn't true!

> Nearly every wife or husband who thinks *My spouse doesn't care* is flat wrong. Their unhappiness is caused by a belief that simply isn't true!

Remember the Person You Married

It seems odd that we even need to ask partners in a marriage to believe that their spouse cares. After all, who gets married assuming that the other person *doesn't* care? But in the day-to-day stresses and strains of doing life together, it's easy to lose sight of that fact.

More destructively, we start believing the opposite. We start gauging the reality of how the other person feels about us, or what that person intended, by *how we feel* in the moment. Do we feel hurt? Well, then, clearly the intention was to hurt us. Or at the bare minimum, the other person just doesn't care enough about us and what we need right now.

But that line of thinking—as understandable as it may be—

is stealing happiness from millions of marriages. One happy wife put it this way:

> The most important factor for a happy marriage is believing that you married a well-intentioned person. It's weird how easily that can go away if you're not careful. We're taught in school and in society to analyze and challenge and have this adversarial mind-set—we forget we are married to these well-intentioned people.

As one longtime family lawyer regretfully told me, "So many divorces could be prevented if people would assume that their spouses had goodwill instead of presuming that they didn't."

One of my all-time favorite academic studies is titled "The Power of Good Intentions," by an assistant professor now at the University of North Carolina.[5] In this study, subjects were given identical electric shocks, but they were told very different things about the partner who was shocking them. Some people were told their partners were being helpful—and were shocking them to help them win money. Another group thought they were being shocked accidentally, without their partners' realizing it. The third group thought their partners were shocking them on purpose, for no good reason.

Consistently, people who thought the shocks were coming

from someone who was trying to be helpful—in other words, those who had good intentions—*actually felt less pain* than those who thought the shocks were accidental or malicious. Remember, the shocks were identical in intensity. But assuming that their partners had good intentions rather than bad ones actually changed the level of perceived pain for participants.

And it works the same way in marriage.

Through the Tunnel and into Green

When it comes to our perception of our spouse's intentions, we really only have two options: we either believe our spouse wants the best for us and we act like it—or we don't.

The either-or nature of this pattern reminds me of a drive I took through the Rockies years ago. My trip started in a beautiful but rather stark area of high desert marked by scrubby bushes and a scattering of pines. Then the highway entered a tunnel in the side of a mountain. Emerging on the other side, I was greeted by one of the most beautiful valleys I've ever seen. Towering aspen, grassy meadows, brilliant flowers, and rushing creeks—what a breathtaking vista greeted my eyes!

The mountains encircling the valley—I later learned— trapped moisture from the air currents that passed over the high desert and turned this hidden place lush and inviting.

It strikes me that in marriage, we are either experiencing one environment or the other, depending on which side we are on. And there's only one way to get into that lush and beautiful valley—to have that abundant Yes! marriage we all desire. You have to go through a very specific tunnel: you have to *believe the best of your spouse even in the darkness.*

Unlike most of the other habits I studied, this one was very nearly a prerequisite for a happy marriage. Either we try to believe the best of our spouse when we are hurt, or we allow ourselves to believe the worst sometimes—which keeps us from ever entering that lush valley where we so want to be.

Now, the sparse side—the side that sometimes doubts the best—can still be beautiful in spots, but it's simply not ideal; it's marked by negative assumptions about our spouse's intentions and feelings. If you're a wife, you might doubt (either subconsciously or consciously) that your spouse really cares about you completely all the time. For example, you worry that he's working so many hours because he cares about work more than about you and the kids. Or you assume that if he feels the pull of Internet pornography, it's because he's not satisfied with you.

For the husband, those negative assumptions might reveal themselves when she points out—again—that your efforts to fix something didn't work, and you conclude that nothing you do will ever be good enough for her. Or maybe when she's contradicting you in front of the kids, you assume she has absolutely no respect for your judgment as a father (and thus that it's best to let her do what she wants to do, since she obviously doesn't care about your opinion anyway).

So if we have fallen into that trap, have forgotten we are married to well-intentioned people, and are on the desert side of the mountain, how can we get back that assumption of goodwill that makes all the difference? How can we go back through the tunnel and into the green?

Many Yes! couples I interviewed had in the past spent time on the desert side of the mountain, and the answer from almost all of them was this: *We must choose to believe it, even if we don't feel it.* Realize that since we are all imperfect beings, we will hurt each other and be hurt by each other—sometimes inadvertently, sometimes out of carelessness (remember Sandy's opening story?), and sometimes even purposefully!

As one husband put it, "Even the best Christian husband or wife can act jerky sometimes, but it doesn't mean they don't love or appreciate you."

Here's how Sandy later described her feelings as she sat alone on the deck that night:

I wasn't upset because I was missing some movie I really wanted to see. I was upset because of what his choices implied about his feelings. The fact that he'd be so cavalier about something that he *knew* was so important to me made it feel like he just didn't care about me— that hanging out with the boys was more important than hanging out with me. But *I know that is not true.* I know he loves me. And, with his mom's passing, he has had an intensely exhausting few months. I know he really did need that time with his friends.

Unfortunately, I needed him too. But even though I didn't get him that night, I know he meant it when he said that he wants and needs to have that time with me. One of my friends said, "He just takes you for granted," but I actually chuckled at that because if ever there were a husband who doesn't take his wife for granted, it would be mine. He demonstrates his love to me in so many ways, little and big. The key is reminding myself of that fact when I'm hurt. I have to go through this process and remember his heart, and then change mine. Just like he has to when I do something to hurt him. (emphasis added)

Notice that in addition to not believing the worst, Sandy took the next—and very necessary—step: she then looked for another explanation for his seemingly uncaring behavior. And anyone can do this. When your man suddenly doesn't seem to want to invest in time at home, maybe it *isn't* that he cares more about work—maybe he is trying to ensure he's not part of the next round of layoffs. When your wife takes the fresh laundry out of your hands and starts refolding it, maybe it *isn't* that she thinks you're incompetent to do it right; maybe she simply has her way of doing it and doesn't realize how her action is coming across.

Looking for a more generous explanation (not an excuse but an explanation) completes the circle and creates a positive cycle. Because once you are willing to look for the truth rather than being blinded by your hurt feelings, you start to see, each time, *that you were right to assume the positive.* ("Wow...now that we've talked, it's clear that she would not have done that if she had known how much it would sting.") Suddenly your heart toward your spouse changes. And once that happens over and over again, you become fully convinced—subconsciously *and* consciously— that your spouse is for you and wants your best, even when he or she does something that hurts, frustrates, bewilders, or angers you.

> Once you are willing to look for the
> truth rather than being blinded by your
> hurt feelings, you start to see that you
> were right to assume the positive.

Over and over, as I interviewed happy couples, I would hear comments like these:

- "He's a pretty direct person, and since this is my second marriage, I'm a bit jumpy. But I've seen what is in his heart for me. So when something comes out of his mouth that is sharp, it can still hurt, but I know he doesn't mean for it to. So it doesn't hurt for long."

- "Why am I so happy? I remember that no matter what I hear, what I feel, what may happen, Paula has my best interests at heart."

- "We are happy because I simply don't question his motives. I may disagree with how he *handled* something and think he's totally wrong and I'm right, but I don't question his actual motives!"

- "I was so mad. I was expecting her to be in my corner, and she disagreed with me instead. But I forced myself to think about it, and three minutes later, I realized that she was so right. The reason I could take it from her is that I know her heart for me is good. She can say anything because of that."

One of the reasons these men and women were so happy in their marriages is that they had all gone through the tunnel and were firmly in the abundant place of believing that their spouses cared about them, regardless of the situation. More important, they weren't being naive. As you saw from the survey results earlier, they were, in fact, correct in that assessment!

And thankfully, happy couples assured me that there's more good news: once you believe your spouse absolutely cares about you, those distancing feelings of hurt, anger, and resentment arise *a lot* less often.

> Once you believe your spouse absolutely cares about you, those distancing feelings of hurt, anger, and resentment arise *a lot* less often.

Expecting the Best Brings Out the Best

The choice to believe the best about your spouse may not come easily at first. You may know in your head she appreciates you, but your heart is still stinging from the way she just teased you at the dinner party about having to call the plumber because you weren't able to fix the faucet.

But the most important step isn't to simply push away those negative feelings; it is to respond as if the most generous explanation is the true one. Do that and you'll find that it is suddenly easier to respond well—because if she just didn't realize how her words would hurt you, then you find your anger draining away and you respond gently. You will automatically prevent the negative downward spiral that would be so easy to start.

And even better, if you're like most of the couples I interviewed, although the choice to believe in your spouse's goodwill may start out being difficult, it quickly becomes natural. You start to see and live by the truth of the matter. And a positive spiral starts instead.

As one older husband, married forty-eight years, put it, "Why *wouldn't* I believe that she has good intentions toward me? Just from a purely personal-interest standpoint, I want to get along with everybody. It's a no-brainer to *want* to expect the best because it increases the chances that I'll get the best. I certainly won't go in looking for something wrong. Instead, I take something she says that is a bit shaky, and I decide to interpret it well. Because otherwise, if I go in suspicious and she says something shaky, I'll probably take it all wrong."

His wife interrupted. "And that is why our marriage is so successful. That's why he was so successful with kids as a counselor for so many years. By going in expecting the best, he brings out the best."

By expecting the best, you bring out the best. That's a great summary. I believe everyone knows that, deep down. We just have to act on it. And when we do, everything changes.

Survey Says

Do you care about your spouse and want the best for them, even during painful times?

	Highly Happy Couples	Mostly Happy Couples	Struggling Couples
Yes, absolutely.	99%	97%	80%
Yes, sometimes.	1%	3%	17%
These days, not really.	0%	0%	3%

Nationally representative and churchgoers' results combined.

Is the following statement true or false? "Even in the middle of a painful argument, I know that my spouse is fully 'for me' and deeply cares about me."

	Highly Happy Couples	Mostly Happy Couples	Struggling Couples
Yes, that is mostly true.	96%	87%	59%
No, that isn't really true for me.	4%	13%	41%

Nationally representative and churchgoers' results combined.

Highly Happy Couples

Go to Bed Mad

Why Sleeping on It Might
Be Smarter After All

One of the fun things about doing this research with happy couples over the last few years was uncovering what a highly happy couple actually *did* as opposed to what they thought they *should do* (and sometimes, even what they advised others to do). Because occasionally there was an amusing disconnect.

The first time I stumbled across this was early in an interview with a couple who wanted to share their top three pieces of advice for a happy marriage. Our conversation went like this:

Him: One big thing is to not go to bed mad.

Her: Don't hold on to things overnight. One of our
        verses is "Do not let the sun go down on your
        anger." And we've maintained that. If we have a
        disagreement, we don't go to bed. It's important.

Me: Yes. So do you ever go to bed mad?

(Pause)

Her: Well, I mean, it's a really important principle.

Me: Absolutely. But do *you guys* ever go to bed mad?

Him: Oh, well…you know…it is a habit you have to
        build. We help our pastor by doing some premarital
        counseling, and we tell young couples—

Me: Yes, sorry to interrupt, but what I'm curious about
        isn't the overall principle, but whether *you two* ever
        go to bed mad. *You, specifically.*

(Pause)

Him: Well [wry look], every now and then.

Her: Most of the time we try to resolve it. We do think
        it is important. But it's just not always possible.

Him: Frankly, if it is late at night, I'm fried. I can't even
        think. Yeah. We try. But sometimes we do agree
        that we will not finish this now and will pick it up
        tomorrow. And sometimes things go a lot better in
        the morning.

You'll be interested to know that this conversation was highly representative of others I had with many dozens of happy husbands and wives. What they at first *said they did* about conflict at bedtime, what they nearly always *advised others to do,* and what they mostly *believed they should do* simply did not jibe with *what they had actually proven in experience works best.*

I know—you're already reaching for your Bibles. I did too. But if you're willing to listen to what happy couples have learned to *actually do,* and take a fresh look at that well-known "do not let the sun go down on your anger" Bible verse, I think your relationship will change for the better.

When Later Beats Now

The habits of the Yes! couples were clear on the survey: When there is conflict and anger that cannot be easily resolved, the think-about-it-overnight option is quite common—and doesn't seem to lessen the strength of their marriages at all. In fact, as you'll see, it may even preserve a marriage!

Let's take a look, starting with the surprising finding I've been referring to. I asked the three categories of couples—highly happy, mostly happy, and struggling—a question: "Many couples have heard that it's important to not go to bed mad. When you and your spouse get into an emotional conflict and at bedtime it is still unresolved, how do you actually handle it?"

Looking at the combined survey results (see the end of the chapter), what I find remarkable is that couples in all three categories agree that resolving anger before bed is a good idea. Yet more than half the time, they go to bed with the conflict unresolved. Is this wrong? I suppose it *could* be—but even for highly happy couples (since they're still highly happy after plenty of experience going to bed mad), it seems to work just fine.

The most noteworthy finding by far in this data can be seen in the differences among those who said that they go to bed with it unresolved, and it remains unresolved (see the graph below). When the struggling couples go to bed mad (and nearly 94 percent of them do), *41 percent don't resolve it later.* Put another way,

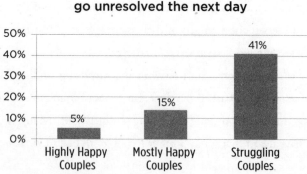

Percent of couples who let conflict go unresolved the next day

struggling couples are *eight times more likely* to say "Once we go to bed with it unresolved, we tend to just not deal with it later, and it remains unresolved."

The difference, then, is not in what couples believe or even do on the evening of the conflict. The difference is what happens later. Just 5 percent of highly happy couples let a conflict go unresolved. Yes, they were okay with sleeping on it, but if the disagreement still seemed important the next day, they dealt with it.

This brings us to the full statement of our surprising secret for this chapter:

Highly happy couples find that when they can't resolve conflict and anger before bedtime, they choose to sleep on it. If anger remains in the morning, they don't let it go unresolved; they deal with it.

Although many Yes! couples mentioned the scriptural advice to never "let the sun go down on your anger" (which they translated as "don't go to bed mad"), *in practice* these couples didn't always follow their own advice! Why? Because they had found that *not* trying to fully resolve conflict at bedtime sometimes allowed them needed emotional space and actually helped boost marital happiness.

In fact, many of the happiest couples reported that trying to resolve all conflict before bed can sometimes be hurtful. As one spouse put it, "Trying to force it can make it worse when you have two upset, tired people trying to hash something out at three o'clock in the morning."

> Happy couples found that not trying to fully resolve conflict at bedtime sometimes allowed them needed emotional space and actually helped boost marital happiness.

Another said, "You do sometimes reach a point, late at night, where you know nothing good is going to come from this point on and it's better to have some processing time. That's bad if it's a long-term avoidance tactic, but good if it's self-awareness that we'll get a better result tomorrow."

Especially since, as his wife chimed in, "We sometimes find that it doesn't even really matter tomorrow! Sometimes we are so put out with one another, and the next morning, we're like, 'Why were we so mad about this?' and we figure it out in five minutes."

Bottom line: instead of sticking to a rule about anger having to be resolved before a given time of night, the rule the happy couples stuck to was to *not* let stuff build up that would ultimately make them unhappy with each other later.

> Instead of sticking to a rule about anger having to be resolved before a given time of night, the rule the happy couples stuck to was to not let stuff build up that would ultimately make them unhappy with each other later.

Knowing this secret of happy couples is critical, since I frequently see young couples unintentionally hurting each other or their relationship because they've been told it is so dangerous to go to bed mad. So when it gets late and the argument isn't resolved, one or both spouses feel panicky about needing to resolve it *right now*. Or, the next morning they feel so guilty that they didn't.

As one young wife told me, "I start to worry that 'We aren't doing marriage right!' So I can't afford to let him have space, because we can't let the sun go down on our anger!" I have seen cases where this concern starts an unnecessary cycle of pressure and even recriminations that can be much more damaging than the original conflict.

It would be great to take the pressure off well-intentioned couples who secretly worry they are setting themselves up for failure when, in fact, they may be reacting and handling things in a very healthy way.

Where's the Verse That Says "Sometimes Things Go Better in the Morning"?

Now, if you care as much as Jeff and I do about following biblical teachings in marriage, I'm guessing you're hoping I'll now produce a helpful verse you've never noticed before. One that says something like "Sometimes things go better in the morning."

But since there is no such verse, let's instead take a look at the biblical texts that do exist, and which most commonly inform Christian marriage advice on this topic. One church leader I was talking to pulled up two key Bible verses side by side on her tablet, like this:

Be angry, and yet do not sin; do not let the sun go down on your anger. (Ephesians 4:26)	Don't sin by letting anger gain control over you. Think about it overnight and remain silent. (Psalm 4:4)

She pointed out that each admonition has the same first half but different second half. One seems to say don't wait. The other seems to say waiting might be a good idea.

"Honestly," she said, laughing, "everyone quotes that second part of the Ephesians verse as if it were some flat-out rule. But the common denominator in the scriptures is the point about not letting anger get the best of you. If you need to stay up to tussle it out before you go to bed so you don't hurt the other person in your anger, do it. But if you need to shut up and get some space and think about it overnight for you to respond well, do that."

I took the same question to Erik Sundquist, a respected leader in Christian counseling and the national director of Safe Harbor Christian Counseling. He provided another reassuring perspective. Here's what he said about the oft-quoted verse from Ephesians:

> Everything I know about interpreting the Bible makes me think that that passage doesn't mean you have to resolve something before you see the orange ball dip below the horizon. It means, in general, that when you see conflict, forgive! Resolve!
>
> The problem is that when it is late at night and one person needs time to process and doesn't get that time, it puts them at a disadvantage. You're trying to have this conversation and the other person doesn't have their feet on the ground to figure out what they are feeling. I see this with men, especially, all the time. It is not a level

playing field for the one who needs to think it through
first.

So if you need to, it is usually okay to wait until both
people know what they're thinking and feeling. And in
most cases, you'll usually have much better communication in the morning.

In all these conversations about processing anger according
to biblical guidelines, an important distinction surfaced. Happy
couples had discovered the difference between resolving their
anger and resolving the *issue*. In practice, they would try especially hard to talk through or deal with their anger or hurt feelings before bed, even if the issue itself wasn't resolved.

> Happy couples discovered the
> difference between resolving their
> *anger* and resolving the *issue*.

It wasn't always possible, of course, but even a little bit of
forgiveness or reconnection sometimes made a difference. "There's
a difference between resolving your conflict and having anger
about it," one experienced marriage mentor told me. "The biblical
principle of 'do not let the sun go down on your anger' doesn't

mean we always agree or reach agreement. It's that we try to not have anger about it. If we can. Because that is where the devil will try to get you."

Getting clarity on this issue is a huge unburdening for many couples. Once, in front of an audience of five hundred women at a church conference, I asked, "How many of you have heard that it is really important to not go to bed mad or to not let the sun go down on your anger?"

Nearly every hand went up.

"Now let me ask, in your own marriages, how many of you have sometimes ended up just deciding to go to bed when you're angry and to deal with it in the morning instead?"

There was a long pause as the women looked at one another. Then, sheepishly, a few hands poked up. I waited. Slowly, others raised their hands until only a small number hadn't. Yet *nearly every woman looked a bit shamefaced and on edge.*

"Guess what?" I said, grinning. "Most of the happiest couples do that too!"

An explosive sigh of relief swept the auditorium as the women exhaled and relaxed in their seats. Finally they could believe their marriages weren't on the road to failure simply by (gasp!) sometimes going to bed mad and dealing with the issue in the morning.

Extending Grace in Our Differences

Would I have heard that same collective gasp from a room full of men? Honestly, I doubt it, and here's why.

According to both brain science and the surveys I did for *For Women Only* about the inner lives of men, men will usually want and need more time than women to process unwanted feelings—and will need to think it through internally instead of talking it through. Thus in a nighttime emotional disagreement, a thoughtful husband is quite likely to want to think things through overnight. First, so he actually knows what he feels; and second, so he doesn't let hurtful things fly in the heat of the moment.

By contrast, it's far more likely that the wife will be the one who wants to keep talking, no matter how late. She needs to work through her unwanted feelings and come to the reassurance that "We're okay" before she can let it go enough to sleep.

As one husband summarized, "I tend to go to bed with a clearer mind than she does because I *know* that eventually we'll be okay and in the morning we'll reconnect just fine because we got a good night's sleep. That is typical for men. But women worry about it and process it while they lie there in bed. They want a clear mind, but they can't until they have resolution."

Ultimately, in Yes! couples, both spouses were willing to

hang in there and pursue something before bed *or* to wait until the morning, if doing either mattered a great deal to their spouse. The key ingredient was trying—if possible—to reach what one husband called "relational peace."

One happily remarried husband told me, "Once my brain has gone fuzzy, I'll still try to invest a little more since she wants to get it resolved, and on her part she'll understand we may not be able to. But we'll at least recognize where we are and affirm that things will be okay."

His wife agreed. "One of the things we're trying to work on is to say we can't fix all this right now," she said. "But we can reassure each other before we go to bed that we are committed. Knowing we'll be okay is what is important."

> "We can reassure each other before we go to bed that we are committed. Knowing we'll be okay is what is important."

To Become One Again

As you move forward, perhaps you can experiment with emulating these happy couples who sometimes *don't* push for resolution late at night, agree to tackle it in the morning if necessary, and reassure each other that they are committed. I hope this chapter has reassured you that if you already do this, it may be healthy rather than the destructive pattern you may have feared. Because ultimately, the right pattern is whatever will bring you back together in unity.

One day as I was finishing up the interviews for this book, I was talking to a senior pastor with whom I have worked intensively over the years. Because I respect him so much, I asked him for his perspective on the "do not let the sun go down" passage. I wanted to know, What is *the* most important issue: that timing, or resolving your anger?

He thought for a moment, then gave his answer, which I think is profound:

Quite simply, that verse keeps the pressure on. We may not resolve it by end of day, but it motivates us to move back to oneness. When I go to bed ticked off, I'm not happy. So I may be fresher in the morning, but it is an unhappy fresher. It leads me to not want to do that again. It leads me to want to do whatever we need to do, to at least not be angry overnight, the next time. To become one again. Because once you've tasted that oneness, you can't live without it.

Survey Says

Many couples have heard that it's important to not go to bed mad. When you and your spouse get into an emotional conflict and at bedtime it is still unresolved, how do you actually handle it?

	Highly Happy Couples	Mostly Happy Couples	Struggling Couples
We keep working to resolve it; we always resolve our disagreements before we actually go to sleep.	20%	10%	4%
Although we think that resolving it before bed is a good idea, it doesn't always work out that way; we sometimes resolve it later—or it ends up not being as important in the morning.	60%	68%	52%
Once we go to bed with it unresolved, we tend to just not deal with it later, and it remains unresolved.	5%	15%	41%
This doesn't really apply to us; we rarely have this type of emotional conflict.	15%	7%	2%

Note: Due to rounding, some percentages do not total 100%.

Nationally representative and churchgoers' results combined.

Keep Score

How What You Count Up Changes What You Give Back

You can tell a lot about a couple by what they argue about. And at least in our marriage, what Jeff and I sometimes argue about is, it turns out, a good thing.

I couldn't be more serious. Take the little push-and-pull that came up between us one evening a while back.

It had been an unusually long day of work for both of us. At nine thirty, I finally wrapped up my last task and headed downstairs to the kitchen. That's when I heard an unmistakable sound—the clothes washer being turned on.

Sure enough, I found Jeff in the laundry area surrounded by

piles of clothes, ready to start four loads. Just the sight of all the undone family stuff and my husband gamely trying to prevail sent waves of guilt over me. I walked up and gave my man a big hug. "I'm so sorry I haven't done any laundry lately," I told him. "You've done it all. Thank you so much!"

He looked at me in disbelief. "What do you mean *you're* sorry? You've been the one busting your tail. This is the least I can do."

"Yeah," I said, plaintively, "but you're in the last stages of your business launch. And you're helping the kids with their homework. And now you're down here doing *the laundry*!"

"Oh, such a hardship duty that is," he said, chuckling. "You've been on the road, on airplanes, getting no sleep."

"Sure, but *you* haven't been getting any sleep either!" I was feeling a little irritated now. "You've been up until midnight working with the guys lately, *and* you've been carrying the load around here!" This was an argument I didn't intend to lose.

And then I started laughing. Here we were late at night, surrounded by the undone duties of family, bickering over whether the other person was doing more.

It reminded me of that familiar event when two people approach a doorway at the same time: "You go first," says one.

"No, *you* go first," says the other.

"No, I insist!"

Yep, at least on that evening, that was Jeff and me contending for the least favored position—only with stacks of dirty clothes.

Now, obviously that was not a real argument. (We have plenty of those too.) But at that moment it occurred to me that something we were doing perfectly mirrored what Yes! couples described, which is an important adjustment to some very common marriage advice.

The Canoe Theory of Marriage

When Jeff and I got married, we frequently heard "Do not keep score!" And you have probably heard the admonition many times too. What people mean is that keeping a record of wrongs doesn't work in love and marriage. And that is absolutely true. The research was stark that counting your grudges makes you unhappy and cripples any relationship.

But I discovered that Yes! couples absolutely do keep score— they just do it differently. Consciously or subconsciously, partners in highly happy marriages *keep score of what they "owe" their spouses.*

These spouses are *very* aware of what their mates are doing and giving, of how hard their spouses are working to support the family, or how much they try to be good partners. They are highly aware of times when their mates are working longer than normal hours or have had a harder than usual time with the kids. And as a result of this hyperawareness of how much their spouses are giving, they make small but powerful adjustments.

They compensate by giving more—and they never think of it as generosity. They are so aware of what their partner has given that they feel, as many told me, "It's the least I can do." So here's our secret:

Happy spouses keep track of what their mate is giving and what they need as a result, and deliberately try to give back.

One friend calls it the Canoe Theory of Marriage. In their relationship, he says, it's as though he and his wife are out in a canoe, trying to get across the lake. When one paddler is tipping left, the other automatically tips right so they don't tip over.

And the impact of keeping score of the good is hard to overstate. Yes! couples trade a sense of entitlement (*My spouse owes me!*) for a sense of indebtedness that makes them not just willing but *eager* to do whatever they can to give back and serve the other.

Here's one everyday example I heard: For Mary, an emergency-room medical technician, work demands run in cycles. For several months, she finds herself at the hospital most waking hours.

Then demands change, and her hours on duty return to something more reasonable. Mary told me that during her busy weeks, her husband tries to do many of her chores around the house. So once her schedule eases, she deliberately tries to compensate by giving back in some way. When I asked her what that looked like, she shrugged. "Oh, I don't know, exactly," she said. "I just try to do the stuff that is meaningful to him. Like, I'll encourage him to go hunting with his buddies. Or I'll make him his lunch so he doesn't have to make it. Or lots of thank-you sex—that always seems to work well!"

I had to laugh—but I heard similar reports over and over. One reason the happy couples are so happy is that instead of keeping score of how much *they* are doing—and feeling resentful because of it ("I can't believe I'm doing all the laundry")—they instinctively put more energy into keeping track of what *the other person* is giving.

> One reason the happy couples are so happy is that instead of keeping score of how much *they* are doing—and feeling resentful because of it—they instinctively track what *the other person* is giving.

Choosing to Keep Score,
Then Compensating

You're going to see in the research results on this issue (see Survey Says section) that twice as many Yes! couples as struggling couples said their partners would notice and compensate for a time when things were off balance. We asked, for example, "If you did all the chores your spouse usually does—for a week or two while he or she was extra busy at work—would your spouse notice and compensate for that in some way? (By being extra nice and thankful, taking you out for dinner, giving you a break in turn, etc.)"

In fact, nearly two-thirds of happy spouses said that their partners would, without being nudged, notice and compensate for a time when things were off balance, where only a third of struggling spouses said the same.

And then there's the disheartening combined statistic that for almost half of all struggling couples, the clueless spouses either won't help compensate in a time of clear need or won't even notice.

As you look at this, you might have several thoughts. You might protest, *Well, if my spouse were to chip in when we've been off balance, I'd be happy too!* But remember something very important: the survey included the answers of *both spouses*. Which means that among the struggling couples, both partners were often answering the same way. In other words, if this is your situation, your spouse probably thinks you don't compensate either!

This brings us back to the paradox that if you will focus on what *you* can do to serve your spouse during their busy times, without worrying if they do the same, you're not only likely to be happier, but you're also likely to see your spouse's pattern change over time.

> If you will focus on what *you* can do to serve your spouse during their busy times, without worrying if they do the same, you're not only likely to be happier, but you're also likely to see your spouse's pattern change over time.

But perhaps you have a different protest. Perhaps you think, *Look, some people are just more observant and helpful by nature. They simply always pay attention to who's doing what and compensate automatically. Goody for them…but that's just not me.*

I wondered about the "it's just their personality" premise too—but I actually discovered something quite the opposite. At the start, this "canoe" behavior didn't come any more naturally to the highly happy spouses than to anyone else. The main difference was that certain people *chose* to keep score of what the other person was contributing—they worked at it, in fact—and *chose* to respond. And in time it essentially became a habit…because it delivered such good results!

One Yes! wife described herself as coming from a family that, as she put it, had a "very glass-half-empty outlook." She then laughed ruefully. "Actually, we never saw things as even *half* empty; we'd be convinced it was less than that." She told me how she started keeping score of the good rather than the bad:

> Maybe because of my background, I did keep score of
> all sorts of irritations. It made it hard on us. Like, we'd
> decided I would stay home with the kids. I knew it
> was the right thing to do, but I didn't want to. So I was
> focused on what I was doing, and what he wasn't doing.
> Or what he wasn't doing right.
>
> Then we adopted this dog. And it was not a good
> thing. I was walking this dog one day, wishing we had
> given it back. And I felt like God said, "What can you
> think of about the dog that is good?" I know it sounds
> funny, but it started me on the road of thankfulness.
>
> And then I found myself starting to do the same
> with [my husband] Trey. I would pray for him, but
> instead of praying that he'd do this and this, or that he

would repent for such and such, I would start praying for him by rehearsing the things I was thankful for. I spent time wrestling it out in our living room. I'd be praying so as to *not* keep account of the bad and leaving it to the Holy Spirit to work it out—usually in me, which was really aggravating—or work it out in him.

And then, amazingly, Trey would do something like call in the afternoon to apologize. It really reinforced the need to do all of that. And then that made me want to do things for him, to say thank you.

As this couple soon found, this seemingly small shift—keeping track of the pluses, not the minuses; keeping track of what your spouse is giving, not what you are—very naturally leads to two virtues in marriage that can have radical, long-term, positive impacts.

Two Marriage-Building Virtues That Come from Tracking the Good

The first virtue is *generosity*. As I talked to these couples, I realized that in little and large ways, they were all going against the tide of a culture that says for you to be happy, you need to watch out for yourself—even in marriage—lest you get taken advantage of.

Yes! couples just didn't see it that way. They were keeping track of what they "owed" their spouses, giving back…and discovering that the greatest happiness came when they *didn't* worry about getting taken advantage of. They were choosing instead to notice their spouse's contributions, and—when periods of stress and busyness threatened their mate—take steps to relieve the load. And like Jeff starting on four rounds of laundry late at night, they didn't expect or care to be noticed.

Dr. Brad Wilcox at the University of Virginia conducted a survey (*Survey of Marital Generosity, 2010–2011*), which showed that marital generosity is one of the greatest contributing factors to happy marriages. In one of my interviews with him, he defined *generosity* as being when one partner will simply do nice things for the other, getting nothing in return. He told me,

> In the 1970s, women thought marriage was asking for
> sacrifice from women and not from men. So in the height
> of the "me decade," they threw out the baby with the
> bathwater, threw out the idea of self-giving as an ideal.
> But the idea of being other-oriented is essential. And
> husbands are called to have that approach too. From
> our perspective, the 1970s failed because it stressed the
> importance of seeking your own fulfillment on your

own terms for yourself, whereas marriage is more likely to flourish when husbands and wives see it as an opportunity to serve one another and make a gift of self to one another, which in this study we call marital generosity. And it turns out that both the receipt of *and* the gift of marital generosity are linked to marital happiness. Both receiving regular acts of service from your spouse *and* *giving* regular acts of service to your spouse predict higher levels of happiness for both husbands and wives.[6]

The numbers Dr. Wilcox found are pretty staggering. In a survey of 2,230 married men and women with children, Dr. Wilcox used a similar 1 to 5 marriage-happiness scale as I did, so I partnered with him to see what patterns arose when he grouped respondents in the three happiness categories.[7] On his survey, Dr. Wilcox had asked people what they did for their spouses (not what their spouses did for them) in four simple areas of "daily generosity": performing small acts of kindness, expressing admiration, expressing respect, and forgiving their spouses for something. In looking at the new analysis (see end of chapter), we discovered that the vast majority of those who had high daily generosity were very happy in their marriages, whereas the vast majority of those who weren't as generous were struggling in theirs![8]

Percent of couples with high daily generosity

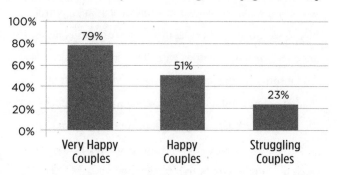

In other words, *people who generously focused on their spouses—rather than on themselves—were more likely to be very happy in marriage!*

Now, you probably know what it feels like to see signs that your spouse is feeling stressed or unhappy, and yet not know what to do about it. It can be awfully tempting to hope it just gets better on its own! One young husband relayed how he kept himself out of that common trap. He explained,

My approach used to be, well, if I see a need or unhappiness and don't say anything, it will go away and that will solve it. But that makes it worse!

When we first got married, we had a period where she didn't work. And she really likes to cook. But then she got a job and was still trying to cook all the meals, and I could see it was wearing on her. At first, I just sat back and was like, "Ah, it'll be okay." But I could see it wasn't. So I suggested that for cooking, I take a week and she take a week. That changed a lot. She told me she was *so* glad that I brought it up since she felt like she couldn't say anything without making me feel criticized for not helping.

She still brings it up today—that that was my best idea ever. Two years later, she still brings it up.

Talk about a little thing that had a big impact.

And it is so important to emphasize, as one happy wife said, that you can't do marital generosity with the expectation of getting something in return. Because that, after all, is negative scorekeeping.

> You can't do marital generosity with the expectation of something in return.
> Because that is negative scorekeeping.

If you would like to experience more marital happiness through generosity but aren't quite sure how to get there, a pivotal point seemed to surface in my interviews. And that brings us to the second virtue.

Many Yes! couples described one crucial change in perspective that almost always caused them to shift from keeping a record of what they were contributing and giving to being very aware of what they "owed" their spouses: they began to recognize that maybe, just maybe, they themselves were in great need of grace. As one husband put it,

> What most people don't recognize enough is how much grace your spouse has to have with *you*. But when you see your own stuff, your own selfishness, that's when you really experience the grace of being loved despite your imperfections. That's when you start to be so grateful for the person who loves and does so much for you anyway. Otherwise, it's like, "Hey! Who wouldn't love me? God is lucky to have me on His team."

Do you see the importance of focusing on what you need to give, rather than what your spouse isn't? Now, I fully realize that there are some sad cases where someone is truly just a lazy, selfish taker who is perfectly fine with their spouse doing it all. But in my interviews, those situations were rare. When I dug deep with a dissatisfied or unhappy spouse, I almost always found that there were plenty of good, generous things their mate was doing that deserved generosity in return…and plenty of things they themselves were doing that warranted forgiveness and grace.

The awareness of those times when our partners really *are* being generous—and when we aren't—is what Yes! spouses learn to focus on. It is a small thing that creates big happiness in our marriages. And the good news is that this is a habit that anyone can adopt.

She Steps Back, He Steps Up

One couple, married forty years, described the give-and-take of keeping score of the good and giving back as a learned skill like ballroom dancing. It was a matter, they said, of staying attuned to where your partner is and what needs to happen next.

Him: It becomes like a dance, where you're each stepping up where the other is stepping back. When work was crazy for her, I was angry at her employer. But then the other part of me went overboard trying to alleviate her stress at home, like stepping it up and cleaning, or doing more pick up and drop off with things she'd promised to do…just meeting her needs and trying to make her life easy…praying with her, and reminding her to keep her work in perspective.

Her: And he always wants to make sure I'm okay, so I want to reciprocate by doing whatever I can do for him and making sure he's taken care of...because he's busy too. I'll make him eat when he's too busy or drive him to and from work so he doesn't have to worry about parking the car in a bad area. Because he takes care of me, it makes me want to take care of him.

Him: We've gotten through so many things in our life, so we're really attuned now to doing things for each other—and doing it together.

If you aren't already, keep an eye out for ways that your spouse is giving and what they need as a result, then try to meet those needs. And stop yourself from wondering when they will reciprocate. After all, you're doing this to give back!

Survey Says

Does your spouse notice and respond when you have given more than your spouse has for a period of time? For example, if you did all the chores your spouse usually does—for a week or two while he or she was extra busy at work—would your spouse notice and compensate for that in some way? (By being extra nice and thankful, taking you out for dinner, giving you a break in turn, etc.)

	Highly Happy Couples	Mostly Happy Couples	Struggling Couples
Yes, if that happens, my spouse will generally notice and compensate for it in some way.	64%	52%	33%
My spouse may not notice, but if I mention it, he or she will generally do something to compensate for it in some way.	22%	23%	16%
My spouse may notice but won't generally compensate for it.	13%	20%	34%
My spouse generally won't notice, and thus won't compensate.	2%	6%	17%

Note: Due to rounding, some percentages do not total 100%.

"Daily generosity," as measured by whether spouses did various small acts for each other.

	Very Happy Couples	Happy Couples	Struggling Couples
High daily generosity	79%	51%	23%
Low daily generosity	21%	49%	77%

Source: Dr. Brad Wilcox, *Survey of Marital Generosity 2010-2011.*
Note: On this survey, answers were separate for husbands and wives.
The wives' answers are shown here. (Husbands' numbers were similar.)

Boss Their Feelings Around

Why Changing What You Do Changes How You Feel

By now I bet you've noticed how many secrets of highly happy marriages seem to cluster around choices—especially choices about what to think and feel toward your spouse.

Let me show you what I mean...

In chapter 3, we saw how very happy husbands and wives *choose* to believe the best about their spouses—even when the evidence is missing, confusing, or at first argues for believing decidedly less than the best.

In chapter 4, we saw how these same couples are willing to go to bed angry sometimes—not because in principle it's always the best way to go, but because in practice it works for them. Why? Because they've *decided* that they will not allow whatever they're feeling at the moment to hurt their marriages or dictate how they'll feel tomorrow.

And, in chapter 5, we saw how they keep score. They *do* keep score, it turns out, but what they *choose* to tally is the good stuff—and then they look for ways to make loving compensation to their spouses whenever possible.

In this chapter we take this issue of choosing one step further—into the somewhat unfamiliar territory of *choosing what you feel*. I'll admit that most of us grew up believing that we don't choose feelings; they choose us. What we feel just *is*—no choice involved. And that is certainly the message we get from our culture. Feelings have their place, absolutely. But life has a way of teaching us that letting feelings run the show leads to all kinds of bad stuff. Yes, I *felt* like yelling at my college roommate for something she did, and it sure felt good at the time…but then it felt pretty bad when it strained a relationship I used to enjoy. My married friend *felt* like sleeping with an old flame…and then found it felt pretty awful to hide this secret from her husband.

We can all come up with examples of how letting our feelings run the show didn't turn out so well. Many of them.

Is there a better way? The answer is yes, and I promise you, highly happy couples have found it—and everyone else can too.

In fact, building this one habit was clearly one of *the* main ingredients of the secret sauce that turned so many of these marriages from ho-hum to highly happy.

Down in the Basement, Something Changes

As one example, listen to what I heard from Nate, who took me step by small step through what could have turned into serious hurt feelings and a big-time conflict with his wife, Liz. Except it didn't.

Nate had been working eighty-hour weeks and had an important business trip looming. Liz assured him she would pick up his dry cleaning for the trip, even after he offered to take care of the errand himself. But the night before his 6:00 a.m. departure, he arrived home late to find no clean shirts and the dry cleaner closed.

Of course, Liz was mortified and apologized multiple times, but that didn't change the fact she had dropped the ball.

"How did you feel?" I asked Nate.

"I was exhausted," he told me, "and already feeling like she didn't appreciate what I was doing, and this just made it worse. I was so angry. I went down to my workshop in the basement and started pounding something."

I asked him to take me through what happened next.

"Well, I was nailing together this cabinet and thinking how angry I was that she forgot since I had asked her *three times*. And then I started to think about how that wasn't completely fair since I knew she had to take the baby to the doctor and it took forever, and then the moment she got home from getting the prescription filled, she had to start fixing dinner. And I started to think about how she always, always makes dinner for all the kids and me *and* juggles a part-time job in the mornings to help us cover expenses. And she's such an incredible mom, and she's always willing to jump to it and help me with things even though she's so busy.

"And I started to think, *This dry cleaning is so minor compared to so many other things she does. I'm so judgmental sometimes…*

"And then I thought, *Why am I being such a jerk?*"

Did you catch what just happened down there in that basement? It had nothing to do with pounding nails and everything to do with what he "started to think"…and then what he *chose* to do about it.

You see, Nate *changed his feelings.* He essentially talked himself out of being mad! What started as understandable frustration and anger morphed—and morphed again—until he was thinking about how great Liz was and about his *own* shortcomings. How did he do that?

By choosing to stop a train of thought that could have caused the conflict to spiral, hurting his relationship with Liz and their potential for happiness.

Stop That Train of Thought!

If Nate seems like a rare bird indeed to you, I've got big news. Nate is just one of hundreds of other happily married people I found who—regardless of age, cultural background, or temperament—*choose to lead their feelings, not the other way around.* The highly happy couples I studied and interviewed had learned that whenever they were dissatisfied (or were at risk of it), they could change their feelings to be happy. Here's their secret:

Highly happy couples quickly stop a negative train of thought or action, replacing unhappy or angry thoughts or actions with positive ones, in order to change their feelings.

The survey results shine some light on how our thinking leads our feelings (not the other way around) and the telling differences between the couples that have learned this powerful habit and the couples that haven't (see the Survey Says section).

Where more than a third of the struggling couples kept

thinking about (fuming about) their annoyance, just 7 percent of Yes! couples stayed caught up in that negative pattern of thought.

Perhaps even more important, almost two-thirds of Yes! couples *forced themselves to stop that train of thought before they got bothered to begin with.* By contrast, only one in four struggling spouses made that choice (see graph).

Percent who stop a negative train of thought to keep from getting upset

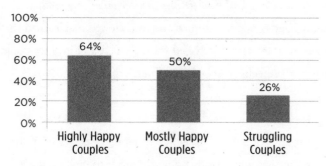

What can we learn? It is apparent from not just the survey but from hundreds of interviews that the more couples choose to stop focusing on and thinking about their annoyance, the happier they will be with their spouses and in their marriages. They will discover we can lead our feelings in a positive direction—*we can actually change how we feel.*

You may wonder, as I did, whether this is realistic to expect of more melancholic personality types, and whether these Yes! spouses are just more likely to have sunny personalities to begin with. But in the end, I found that wasn't the case at all. In fact, while many of the happy spouses certainly did have a glass-half-full personality, many others said the opposite. I was amused, though, at how they described themselves when I asked something like, "Are you more of a glass-half-full or glass-half-empty person?" They would pause, and say gravely, "I would say I'm more of a realist." And yet having discovered the secret that they didn't have to focus on those "realistic" feelings, they were just as likely to be very happy in their marriages. (Including, I might add, my own husband!)

> The more couples choose to stop focusing on and thinking about their annoyance, the happier they will be with their spouses and in their marriages.

Now, it is important to say that this doesn't mean ignoring real issues of concern or pretending that damaging problems don't need to be addressed. But it *does* mean we've got to be careful to address them in ways that add to—rather than hurt—our feelings of goodwill toward our spouse.

Herding Emotions
in the Right Direction

One happy couple emphasized the importance of what they called "herding your emotions" or leading your feelings instead of letting them lead you. I asked what that looked like to them, and the husband responded,

> If there's something my wife has done and I'm angry, I can
> either stew or I can nip it. I can also acknowledge, I may
> be wrong here…or I may actually be right. But either way,
> I can choose to forgive and herd those feelings in the right
> direction. I don't want to stuff those feelings, but I also
> don't want to let them lead me.

This highlights a very important question: Who's the boss—you or your feelings? And how you answer that simple question has pretty big consequences. As King Solomon put it when describing a negative person in Proverbs, "For as [that man] thinks in his heart, so is he."

Sarah, a stay-at-home mom with four young children, described how she sometimes stops a negative train of thought about her construction-worker husband:

When he's been at work all day and comes home
and tells me he needs to take an hour to go drop by
a friend's place to watch the end of the game, I sometimes start to think, *Hey! You're out of the house all day
and don't have to take care of the children! And now to
find out that you want to visit someone? Seriously?* I start
to think, *So when do I get to go out?*

And then I think, *Yeah, but wait. He's been out,
but it's not like he's been with friends—he's been at
work all day! In the hot sun! If I were at work on a site
all day, I would want to have a break to do something
else too.*

So then I'm *glad* there's something he can do to
give him a real break for a few minutes, away from
the kids crawling all over him. Because then I see
how much he needs it, and I want him to get it.

See how that works? Sarah stopped a line of thinking that
was leading to jealousy and resentment. Instead, she began to
think about what it's like in her husband's shoes, on a work site all
day in the heat. She took action to say it was okay that he gets
some downtime. And suddenly, feelings of compassion replaced
feelings of jealousy and resentment. Then Sarah found herself

sincerely *wanting* her husband to get that break and time away, even though she needed time away too.

Sarah put her thoughts and actions, not her feelings, in the driver's seat—and as a result, changed her feelings *and* her thoughts. (And in case you're wondering, Sarah's husband didn't seem like he fit into that small percentage of people who are just insensitive takers. He apparently does make sure she has breaks doing the things *she* enjoys.)

Although the happy couples I spoke with did sometimes need to address perceived imbalances with their spouses, they simply didn't let themselves start the *I'm doing more* or *It's not fair!* train of thought. They understand that that kind of thinking can tear a relationship apart.

Bottom line: these couples have learned *to boss their feelings in the right direction* and in return are receiving a huge happiness payoff in their marriages. And they've learned a key strategy to do it. Beyond simply choosing to think about the positive, they change their *actions*—and find that their feelings follow.

> Beyond simply choosing to think about the positive, happy couples change their *actions*—and find that their feelings follow.

Act as If...and Feelings Follow

During my younger years, I was deathly afraid of flying. It only got worse after an aunt I was very close to was killed in an airplane crash. I explained to people, "I'm afraid of flying, so I'll take the train instead."

Although I prayed for God to take the fear away, nothing changed. One morning at work, as I was prepping for a business trip the next day, I was so nervous about the upcoming flight that I actually felt sick. As I started to express that to a close colleague, the strangest thing happened. I felt as if God were telling me to stop what I was going to say, and instead say, "But I'll be okay because I'm getting over my fear of flying."

The same thing happened that night when I started to tell another friend—and later, Jeff—that I was nervous. It felt as though God brought me up short. Instead of talking about my fears, I felt I was supposed to say "It'll be fine" and "I'm not as afraid anymore"...even though that was not at all how I felt!

By the time I boarded my flight, I was still nervous, but something had changed. I wasn't *terrified*. And believe me, I had been terrified on planes for years. Even more amazing, when my plane had to make an emergency abort of its landing because another plane drove onto the runway, I was okay!

Over the next few years, I realized that God's gentle nudging to stop saying "I'm afraid" and start saying "I'm fine with flying" was what He was using to answer my prayer to make me less afraid!

I was supposed to act as if I were okay, and eventually...I would be. And today, I am!

We Do Have the Power

As I discovered in overcoming my fear of flying, not only does our thinking lead our feelings, but also *our feelings often follow our actions.* We can choose to take positive action—after stopping a negative train of thought, even redirecting it—and choose to speak positively, even if we don't feel like it right at that moment. Basically, we can act as if...

And that's when we discover that because of the way our hearts and minds are wired, we *do* have the power to change our feelings.

You think your wife doesn't appreciate you? Act as if she does...and you'll not only suddenly see evidence of her appreciation everywhere, but you'll start to feel much more affection for her.

You don't really trust your husband's ability to keep the household together while you go on a trip? Act as if you do...and you'll not only see your trust level rising, you might discover that the kids didn't actually fall apart while you were away.

You find yourself incredibly irritated at something your mate just did? Act as if you aren't, and find something you can say "Thank you" for instead…and you'll find the irritation really isn't as big of a deal after all.

And of course—and just as vital—*this applies in reverse as well.* If you find yourself incredibly irritated and you tell your spouse so, and you mention it to your mom, and you complain to your friend at work, you'll find the irritation becoming an even bigger deal in your mind.

Proverbs 11:27 has a great summary of both sides: "If you search for good, you will find favor; but if you search for evil, it will find you!" Ultimately, for better or for worse, it is often our *actions* that end up determining how we feel.

I actually was amused by one particular type of example of this. Several times I conducted scheduled interviews with very happily married couples…who eventually confessed that they had been arguing right before our meeting!

One such couple, on their second marriage, had been seriously at odds in the hour just before we got together. They realized they had drastically different expectations of whether to buy some pricey Christmas presents for her twenty-three-year-old daughter. He explained that he "grew up poor in the 'hood" and rarely got Christmas presents once he was a teenager. She grew up middle class, and he was—as he put it—astonished that "she was still getting Christmas presents when we got married!"

Listen in on the rest of their dialogue with me:

Him: So we were trying to figure out how we do this fairly, and if there even *is* a fair. We got to a point where we were heated and upset with each other, and then we had to leave and go talk about our happy marriage! So we pulled up to the curb here, and I asked, "What are we going to talk about?"

Her: And I said, "We're going to talk about our happy marriage—which we don't have right now! What do we do?" He said, "Let's just pretend." And then he said, "But we *do* have a happy marriage, and it does not depend on how we are feeling right now." That is why we acted as if everything was okay when we came in. We have found that when we act loving, then eventually, wow, we are loving!

> "We have found that when
> we act loving, then eventually,
> wow, we are loving!"

When "Bossing" Makes
for a Sweeter Marriage

My friend Lysa TerKeurst, founder of Proverbs 31 Ministries and a wonderful author and speaker, invited me to write a guest post on her blog about women choosing to believe our husband's love for us instead of allowing ourselves to doubt it. One of her readers posted this comment to me in response, which to me perfectly encapsulates the to-do of this chapter:

> I'm sharing this with my husband tonight—he thinks
> it's just me [that has this doubt]! I've printed it out with
> highlights to remind myself to keep what I'm believing
> in check. *My self-talk has power, and I need to boss it
> around a bit.* (emphasis added)

If bossing your self-talk around sounds more like something you expect to hear in a self-help setting than in a book pointing back to the Bible, consider what the apostle Paul wrote when he was chained to a prison wall: "Rejoice in the Lord always. I will say it again: Rejoice!"

How can we follow this admonition in a difficult marriage or when we're simply having a bad day? The answer comes just a few verses later (you can find this in Philippians 4:8–9): "Whatever is true, whatever is noble, whatever is right, whatever is pure, whatever is lovely, whatever is admirable—if anything is excellent or praiseworthy—think about such things.... And the God of peace will be with you."

> "My self-talk has power, and I need to boss it around a bit."

No waiting around for the mood to strike there! Paul's strong counsel is to *make a decision* to feel and think differently than we might otherwise. That's where change begins.

I understand, of course, that stopping a negative train of thought isn't always easy, especially if you are the only one trying to make things work in a difficult marriage. Those are the times when we especially need God's help and the support of encouraging friends.

But all of us—whether in good relationships or not so good

ones—can *learn* this. As one Yes! wife explained, "Everyone has emotions, and if we're honest with ourselves, we *know* what tends to make us happy and what will lead to a pity party. I *know* that if I start myself thinking *Why can't I have that kind of house?* it is a bad trend, always. Yes, something might cross my path to make me jealous, but at that point I can either focus on it and let it pile on, or I can choose to turn the corner and direct my thoughts in a good way."

As simple as it sounds, if we want to have happy marriages, we must choose to boss our feelings around.

We can't buy into the lie that we are powerless over our feelings. We're not. The Yes! couples show us that we can choose to boss our feelings around and change them in the process. We can choose to be glad instead of allowing ourselves to be constantly dissatisfied. Like so many of the couples who transitioned from struggling to happy, we can choose to focus on whatever is lovely and not on whatever is driving us crazy.

And as we do, we'll start to see the wonderful outcome one husband described: "We think that we'll have to drum up all this willpower and force ourselves to bite the bullet and put on a nice face forever, with no end in sight. But then something changes. I have found that acting it, even though I don't feel it, will make me feel it. And suddenly, it's not acting anymore."

Survey Says

If you were to find yourself thinking that your spouse is doing less or "getting more" than you, which choice best describes what would *most often* happen in your mind?

	Highly Happy Couples	Mostly Happy Couples	Struggling Couples
It bothers me, and I can't help but keep thinking about my annoyance over a period of time.	7%	16%	34%
It bothers me, but instead of thinking about it, I try to stop that train of thought.	29%	35%	40%
I stop that train of thought before I get too bothered to begin with.	64%	50%	26%

Note: Due to rounding, some percentages do not total 100%.

Have Factual Fantasies

How Loving the Art of
the Possible Makes Your
Marriage Stronger

Talk about a storybook marriage—Jake and Lydia have it. When I spent several weeks with them a few years ago, I watched how they interacted and spoke to each other. I saw their unflagging affection and respect for each other. And I came away completely impressed with their relationship.

But I have to admit I was particularly impressed with Jake. He always seemed to know exactly what Lydia needed, and he was sweet, attentive, and understanding. Always. It was amazing.

But even more important, Jake knew what to do when there were conflicts or hurt feelings. Lydia would get insecure and upset, and then she'd pull away. But not Jake. He wouldn't *let* her pull away. He'd say things like, "Honey, I'm not leaving the room until we work this out." Or he would refuse to be deterred by her angry words and simply pull her into a big hug. And of course, since that was what she was secretly wishing for, she would melt.

As I watched how Jake responded to Lydia, I found myself asking why more men couldn't be like that. Even though my husband is wonderful, I hate to admit that I got a little wistful. When Jeff and I are upset with each other, he is the sort to need space right when I most need a hug. So although something in me would be powerfully touched by "I'm not leaving until we work this out," those words don't usually pop up during a conflict!

More worrisome, after spending so much time with Jake and Lydia, I actually found myself becoming a little discontented. Why don't more men see that what a woman needs is for him simply to pursue her, reassure her, and refuse to be deterred? Why can't more men be more like Jake?

Well, there's a good reason.

Jake doesn't actually exist.

You see, Jake and Lydia were characters in an action-romance series I was reading. If you're a man, you probably don't know this, but the main ingredient in any type of romance novel is an admirable and attentive man who pursues a woman past all obstacles. A man who, when confronted by anger, misunderstandings, and tears, says things like "I'm not leaving until we work this out." A man who will overlook his woman's most difficult behavior and pull her into a big, warm hug.

Of course, although that kind of response is what most women instinctively want, and although that type of behavior would be relatively easy for women to do, it is incredibly difficult for men to do. Although every decent husband wants to be his wife's hero, he also often has no idea what he should do when she turns emotional or upset—a confusion he finds very painful. He may not even know yet what went wrong. So his brain is wired to need space to figure it out—especially when he's upset and defensive himself! Regardless, the notion of moving toward his scary, confusing wife is never even going to come up in his mind—or if it does, in the emotional chaos of that moment, it will seem like the *worst* possible idea rather than a good solution.

Thus any woman who thinks *If my husband really loved me, he would act like Jake* is creating a fantasy and an expectation that is completely unrealistic—and she is almost certain to experience disappointment and unhappiness as a result.

In my research, one of *the* main factors that clearly made

couples unhappy was a spouse longing for their mate to deliver something that seems like it should be easy but which their mate finds difficult or impossible.

But when a woman or man instead understands and celebrates the facts of what their partner *can* deliver to meet their needs—when they have factual fantasies instead of unrealistic ones—they completely avoid one of the main causes of unhappiness and are far more likely to enjoy their marriages.

Just the Facts

In my research, it was clear that unrealistic expectations were often incredibly subtle but incredibly widespread. Most couples were laden with them. Most, that is…except the Yes! couples.

Although I found the happiest spouses certainly had high expectations of their mates, they were also (often subconsciously) very realistic. So here's the simple secret we'll be covering in this chapter:

> 💡 Highly happy spouses do not long for something that is difficult or impossible for their partner to deliver; instead they expect and are grateful for the ways their partner *can* meet their needs.

Bottom line, the happiest spouses recognize when their expectations are pure fantasy and stop themselves from thinking things like, *If he really loved me, he would* _____. Instead, they shift to being grateful for the ways their spouses are uniquely wired, and the ways they can and do meet their needs well.

My survey results (see end of chapter) indicate that struggling couples were six times more likely than Yes! couples to be very frustrated or disappointed when their spouses didn't meet their expectations. By contrast, highly happy couples were *twelve times* more likely to say they didn't have those expectations to begin with! (See graph.)

Similarly, nearly half of struggling spouses felt their mates

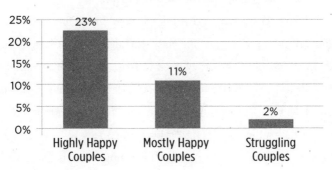

Percent who don't have expectations their spouse doesn't or can't meet

- Highly Happy Couples: 23%
- Mostly Happy Couples: 11%
- Struggling Couples: 2%

had unrealistic expectations of them, where only one in ten Yes! spouses did. (See graph below.)

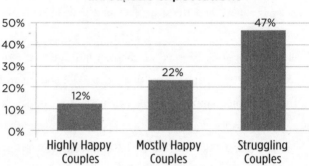

Percent who think their spouse has unrealistic expectations

Do you see the surprising paradox? When expectations just aren't feasible, clinging to that specific ideal of who our partners should be and what they should be able to do actually prevents the ideal relationship that we are longing for.

Don't get me wrong, I think we should have great expectations of our spouse, just like they should be able to have great expectations of us. But they need to be realistic. We are simply foolish to be upset because our spouse didn't do the emotional equivalent of running a four-minute mile! In a culture that seems to put such a high value on storybook romances, we also have to be sure to focus on and celebrate how things work between real men and women in real life.

> When expectations aren't feasible,
> clinging to that specific ideal of what
> our spouses should be able to do
> actually prevents the ideal relationship
> that we are longing for.

Great (Adjusted) Expectations

So how does this play out? Well, it doesn't seem to matter whether our expectations are of the big systemic patterns or about the little day-to-day stuff of life. Realism about *both* are equally important for day-to-day contentment. Listen in on my conversation with a Yes! couple who have counseled many others:

Me: In your experience, if you had to pick one thing that is most likely to make couples unhappy, what would it be?

Him: Hands down, it is unrealistic expectations.

Her: No question. We tell people, "You have subtle expectations from childhood, when you were seeing yourself as a princess married to a prince. You think, *He's going to do this and this and this.* And then when he doesn't, you have resentment. For example, when

I grew up, I saw my dad do things that I assumed all men do. Like mowing the lawn and washing the car once a week. I never thought about it, but I had those expectations whether I realized it or not. So when that didn't happen, it posed problems for me. I began to take it personally!

Him: But in my family we never owned a car. We were poor. That was a source of contention. I couldn't believe she was that serious about her car being washed every week. Or I would take the car to get the oil changed, and she would say, "We can save money if you do it." But I knew nothing about cars! And I had expectations too, but they were totally different. My expectation of her, honestly, was that once we got married, we would make love every single day. I thought it would be really frequent and she would feel like that all the time!

Her: Needless to say, we had some reality checks early on in our marriage.

They went on to say that one of the main secrets to stepping into a great marriage is allowing those reality checks to happen and being willing to adjust one's expectations.

The Genius of Explaining What You Need

Another thing that struck me in my interviews was that the Yes! couples don't just avoid unrealistic expectations about what their mates should deliver—they also help their mates out by explaining what they need! After all, many expectations go unmet not because the other person *can't do* something, but because they *didn't know to do* something!

Many of the less-than-happy spouses I spoke to seemed to think that it didn't count if they had to tell their spouses what they needed.

But Yes! couples totally disagreed.

As one happy husband advised, "It's okay to explain what you want to your spouse. It doesn't lessen the meaningfulness of the act simply because you asked for it. Your partner wants to make you happy—if you make him guess and he gets it wrong, you aren't being fair to him. It's as if you are testing him and almost guaranteeing he'll lose the test. Don't assume he just knows what you need!" Here's a perfect example from one happy wife about what that looks like:

> I went with my husband to his big work convention at a
> resort location. He was worried I would be bored alone in

the room, and since he's an extrovert, he was arranging all these things for me and for our off-hours. Instead of going along with it, I told him, "Honey, please don't. I really need a day in the room. Alone." I'd been on a big work deadline myself, the kids had been sick, and I hadn't had any downtime in months. Instead of holding my tongue and then getting upset that "he didn't know," I specifically told him, "I need *this*."

One very practical wife put it this way: "Why should I be upset when I didn't get what I wanted for my birthday, when I didn't tell him? He would always get me cards and roses; he thought I liked that. So I finally told him, I don't like cards. I don't like roses. But I do like plants I can plant in my garden that come back every year that I can look at and think, *He got me that this year or that year.* And so every year, he gets me a plant, and I have a whole garden full of memories."

The Only Person You Can Change

Ultimately, the happiest couples demonstrate that the main solution to avoiding unrealistic expectations is to focus not on what you wish your spouse would change, but on what *you* can change. As one happy wife of sixty years told me,

There are a lot of people who blame the other person for not doing what they "should" do, rather than realizing that the only person you can change is yourself. We tell people you don't give fifty-fifty. You give 100 percent. Which means sometimes you give in. You adjust your expectations. You uplift the other. You refuse to believe that the other person is undercutting you. You are glad for what your spouse *can* give instead of pouting over what they can't. There are no magic guarantees, but this does seem to be God's way of doing it. And giving up your expectations and your rights usually results in getting back the love you wanted all along.

> "Giving up your expectations and your rights usually results in getting back the love you wanted all along."

The happiest couples take what might seem like the foolish risk of adjusting their expectations to be more factual and adjusting their focus toward what they themselves need to do differently. But what they receive in turn is much more contentment, much less conflict, and a stronger, deeper love. Who wouldn't say the exchange was worth it?

Survey Says

Most spouses have times when they feel frustration or disappointment because their husband or wife did not meet their expectations. When that happens to you, how much does it bother you?

	Highly Happy Couples	Mostly Happy Couples	Struggling Couples
It bothers me quite a bit.	7%	18%	40%
It bothers me some.	39%	48%	35%
It really doesn't bother me at all.	12%	9%	7%
It starts to bother me—but I get a grip, so that it doesn't end up bothering me much.	20%	14%	16%
I don't really have expectations that my spouse doesn't meet, so this doesn't apply to me.	23%	11%	2%

Note: Due to rounding, some percentages do not total 100%.

Do you think your spouse expects some things from you that you feel are difficult or impossible to deliver?

	Highly Happy Couples	Mostly Happy Couples	Struggling Couples
Yes, I do feel that my spouse has some unrealistic expectations of me.	12%	22%	47%
My spouse probably wishes some things were different, but doesn't generally expect things I cannot deliver.	57%	59%	40%
No, my spouse doesn't wish for or expect things I cannot deliver.	31%	19%	14%

Note: Due to rounding, some percentages do not total 100%.

Use Sign Language

How a Silly Signal of
Reconnection Can Bypass
Hurt and Bring Reassurance

think of this as the porcupine problem: How does a couple get close again when one or both spouses have been bristling with hurt feelings and anger?

The answer might be the same one we heard in Zoology 101 for the question, how do porcupines have sex?

Answer: very carefully.

But, seriously. We've all been in one of those prickly situations. Right when we most need to give or receive reassurance that whatever upset we're experiencing now *will not* create the beginning of a problem in our marriages, we can't safely speak to each other. (Maybe we can't stand to be in the same room.)

So what do we do? How do we keep from being one of those couples that just tends to hope that the prickles will be better tomorrow—and yet even when they are, it feels like there's more distance than before?

That's what we'll talk about in this chapter. And you'll be relieved to know that highly happy couples (even when they are porcupines) have instinctively come up with a powerful little solution.

In one of my first in-depth interviews, a Yes! couple took me step by step through a fracas that had occurred a few nights before. Each had hurt feelings, and they had endured a frosty silence for about four or five hours. But listen in on what they said happened next:

Her: So then he came upstairs and we touched pinkies.
       And I told him—

Me: Wait. You *what*?

Her: [Looking embarrassed] We touched pinkies. See,
       we have this thing. When we're irritated with
       each other, after a while one of us will come over
       and [she mimes the action] tentatively stick one
       pinkie out. And if the other person goes, "Oh,

all right," and touches pinkies back, then we're okay.

Him: Sometimes we offer an elbow. If it's been a really bad fight.

Her: Or sometimes the other person will actually say, "I'm not there yet!" And it's like, "Okay, we can wait." But more often than not, we go ahead and touch pinkies, and that's it...we're fine.

Me: What happens next? Do you apologize? Do you talk?

Him: Sometimes. But touching pinkies is sort of the apology, I guess. We're reconnecting. I never thought about it before. But regardless of whether we acknowledge the issue at all, that's what we're doing.

What's going on here? A game with little fingers, or something more?

In this chapter we're going to look at how highly happy couples use a private language (that sometimes doesn't even have words) to make them happier in their marriages—an often-unrecognized habit that any couple can emulate.

It turns out that soon after a conflict and hurt feelings, most Yes! couples use a unique, small gesture to reconnect: a word or action that may seem completely meaningless or even silly to an outside observer. And yet to the two of them, it speaks volumes, providing a familiar path to letting go, to forgiveness after conflict, and to starting over again right.

Don't miss this important distinction: *We're not talking here about resolving the disagreement.* It still may be most definitely *un*resolved. Instead, we're talking about a kind of lovers' bypass—a way around all that difficult stuff that gets right to the heart of the relationship and gives it a sort of reassuring hug. The secret of highly happy couples is this:

> When highly happy couples inevitably experience hurt feelings and conflict, they will at some point mutually reconnect by sharing a private signal that says "We're okay."

I'll tell you right up front that discovering this powerful secret was one of my personal research favorites—maybe because Jeff and I had already been doing this without realizing it!

But once my eyes were opened to the Yes! couples' practice of using sign language, I began to notice the pattern everywhere. Unlike many other couples, the Yes! couples had somehow realized the power of reaffirming the *relationship* even if the *issue* wasn't yet resolved. Often subconsciously, they had developed and were regularly using a private way of telling each other "We're okay."

A Private Signal That Says "We're Okay"

Whether or not couples *did* reconnect in this way, everyone seemed to have the *need* to reconnect, to have the *feeling* that "We're back to being okay." Here's how one happy couple put it:

Her: Reconnecting is a real need for me. I do *not* like having the thick air in the house where it goes on for days. It's like relational smog. It feels bad, and it's bad for you.

Him: So for us, we'll crack a joke to clear the air. We generally like being around each other and like each other's company. If I can't be that way with her, it kind of stinks. We have to clear it up.

And the responses on the combined survey show exactly how important this is for happiness in marriage. Fully 70 percent of Yes! couples purposefully reconnect using a mutual signal, compared to only 22 percent of struggling couples. (See graph.)

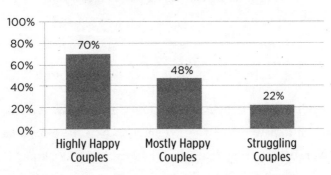

Percent who purposely signal each other that "We're okay" after conflict

Now look at the mostly happy couples for a minute, whose responses landed squarely in the middle of those two extremes. Here is another example of that surprisingly wide gap between the habits of highly happy and mostly happy couples—and an opportunity to help turn those good marriages to great.

This leads us to the very important takeaway of this chapter: almost any couple can increase their mutual enjoyment rather quickly by following conflict with a shared signal that both partners know means "We're okay."

So Many Ways to Say "I'm Sorry"

The options are nearly endless. Highly happy couples told me they accomplish reconnection in so many different ways—everything from a joke or signal that only made sense to them to a straightforward question like "Are we okay?" Here is a sampling of what I heard:

- "He'll say, 'First the Fat Boys break up and now this.' You know that line from the Chris Rock movie? It means nothing. But when things are just piling on and we're upset, that's our joke that clears the air."

- "Uh, yeah." [Looking embarrassed] "She meows at me. I have to meow back."

- "There is always some type of physical touch involved with reconciliation. A kiss, a hug—maybe when I'm driving I'll reach across to take her hand. A sign or something that it's okay, we're okay."

- "I try to stay mad at him, but there's something that only we will laugh at and he knows exactly how to do it, so he cracks me up."

- "One of us will reach over and touch the other person's foot in bed. If they touch back, we're good."

- "I come down the stairs and say, 'Hug me.' Or sometimes he says, 'Hug me.' Whenever there is an argument, there is some type of physical affection that seals the deal to move on. It's the closure. I never thought about it, but I like it that we do that."

- "We get in each other's faces and one of us grins and says, 'You know what? We deserve each other.' And usually, given what we've just exchanged, that is so true. We are such fallen human beings. It's not that one of us is the poor suffering victim and the other's the awful person. Nope, it really puts it on a level playing field and says we were *both* wrong in how we handled it."

- "Definitely hugging and asking, 'Are we good?'"

- "I'll get mad, go off, think about it, come back, say, 'I'm sorry. Are you done being mad now?' Then she'll say, 'I never was mad.' And I say, 'Liar.' I can't explain it, but that gets us back on the same page."

- "We bump each other…like bumper cars around the house. I know—it's juvenile! But if he comes up and bumps against me at the kitchen sink and then a minute later I bump into him in the doorway to the study, I've just said I accept his apology."

- "Sex. Yeah. We talk about it, and then at the end we say, 'I love you,' and then she rips my clothes off…and we're fine. That works for every guy I know."

To be sure, for some couples, their sign language is actually words, not actions. They need to say and hear the words of reconnection—including explicit affirmations of commitment.

> "We're like bumper cars around the house. I know—it's juvenile! But if he comes up and bumps against me at the kitchen sink and then a minute later I bump into him in the doorway to the study, I've just said I accept his apology."

One Yes! husband and wife I interviewed, who were each on their second marriage, told me that they had realized how important it was for them to *say* it:

Him: We do it consciously; we reconnect on purpose. At the beginning of our relationship, that wasn't the case. It was very difficult to feel like it was safe. But lately, the last year or two, we've been able to come together a lot quicker.

Me: How do you do that? What does it look like?

Her: I'll go in and sit on his lap in his office, and just sit there. Or make some physical touch that signals that I'm making the initiative. Every now and then he says, "I need more time," and that's okay. But mostly, when he wraps his arms around me, it signals something.

Him: Then, we specifically tell the other person that we love them and that we're committed. We say the actual words, like, "I'm not going anywhere," or "We'll work this out." It doesn't mean that one of us isn't still working through their feelings and hurts, but it gives the other person the sense that we're still processing and everything's gonna be okay.

Her: It's like a big long exhale for one of us to say those words out loud. Those words are like a little harbor. We can step back and know we're okay—we're not going anywhere.

Letting Reconnection Happen

One reconnecting-after-conflict pattern I noticed on the combined survey was that Yes! spouses were far more likely to let their mates apologize to them or reconnect with them, or both, in this way. One happy husband put it this way: "If we're coming to bed mad, I don't want that. I want to apologize. So if we're upset with each other, I will try to hug her. And even if she's angry or hurt, she'll let me do that. And when I fall asleep holding her, I feel like we're one."

By comparison, if struggling spouses approached their loved

ones to try to make up, they weren't sure if their apology would be accepted—or they actually knew the attempted apology would *not* be accepted (which of course made them less eager to try to reconnect at all).

Seven out of ten Yes! spouses said that if they took the initiative to reach out or apologize, their mate would generally soften or apologize in turn—but only a third of struggling spouses had that same confidence.

In fact, by contrast, nearly six out of ten struggling spouses said they knew their mate *wouldn't* respond in the way they were hoping for, or they wouldn't be able to predict their response.

If you look at the second set of survey results at the end of the chapter, you will notice that the mostly happy couples were, again, squarely in the middle. Both that outcome and the rest of the results imply a great opportunity to increase happiness not only by reaching out to reconnect but also by being sure to welcome that reconnection request when it comes our way. And all of us can certainly do this. We can choose to *not* hold our displeasure over our spouse's head when they do try to reconnect with us.

> We can choose to *not* hold our displeasure over our spouse's head when they do try to reconnect with us.

Finding Our Own First Step

Another reason these steps of reconnection seem to be so important is that, by their very nature, they usually start with just one person taking a step of humility and ownership—*a first step that then softens the heart of the other*. This does not suggest that anyone be a pushover. It suggests the need for changing how your heart feels toward your spouse before you address an issue so that you address it in a way that helps rather than hurts both of you.

I was talking about my research findings with another female author and friend, and when I came to this subject, she chuckled. "I have always told young women that action precedes emotion," she said. "You have to do the right thing even when you are spitting mad and don't feel like it. My husband and I have this custom that at some point before we go to sleep, I will scratch his back. To him, it has come to mean love. Well, what happens when we go to bed mad and we are lying there, furious, back to back?"

She leaned forward, cocked her eyebrow at me, and raised her hand as if it were a claw. "Sometimes I'm so mad I just want to reach over and take these fingernails and draw blood!" She smiled sheepishly. "When we were younger, I *knew* I was supposed to reach over and gently scratch his back anyway—and I would lie there and say, 'I'm going to do that when you-know-where freezes over!' But all that happened was that I was miserable. So I started to force myself to do what I knew I should do. Today, I will force myself to turn over and gently scratch his back. It may take me forever, but I do it. And as a result, 100 percent of the time, I soften toward him. And the next morning, he's softened. One of us knows we need to go with what's right, not what we feel."

It was oddly encouraging for me to see that, like many others, some Yes! couples needed some time before they could reconnect. It wasn't a marriage killer to have a period of angst (although it was rare for them to allow hard feelings to go on for more than twelve to twenty-four hours). The pattern that mattered wasn't the absence of conflict or hurt feelings, but the need, as one man put it, "to rush toward reconnection" so that the husband and wife weren't on the outs with each other for too long.

Forgiveness with a Mug of Coffee

Ultimately, our personal signal of reconnection begins in forgiveness. Not just forgiveness offered or asked for, but forgiveness accepted. The issue doesn't have to be resolved, and we don't have to be all happy-happy right then, but we *can* show that—down deep where it matters—we're okay. The reconnection is not always easy—sometimes we just have to choose—but it does appear to be vital to a happy, abundant marriage.

I'll leave you with this wonderful excerpt from my interview with a couple who have been married for more than thirty-five years:

> We do reconnect. We didn't used to. We used to be so angry with each other. We would try to decide "Do we want to stay in this or don't we?" I had to come to the conclusion that it didn't have anything to do with feelings of love at that point. I started thinking, *Either I can accept him the way he is and be patient with him, or I move on.* And then I started going back to church and getting in with others who were sticking with it, and I realized "moving on" wasn't an option. And I saw how much happier they were because it wasn't. I also saw what God really asks. *Forgive. Lay aside your pride.* I realized I had to make a conscious decision to forgive.
>
> There was a day I just wanted to leave, but he wanted me to come back inside. He was holding out a mug of coffee. And reaching out and taking it was a struggle, but because of my faith, I knew it was the right thing to do. Now, I did have to see in him that he was willing to change and get himself right too, which over time he was.
>
> But the next time I was furious and just wanted to stomp away, I looked at that coffee mug and went to get

it, then held it out to him. And he took it. And we started talking. Now we just pantomime holding out the coffee mug, and the other person reaches out to take it. That's how we started rebuilding. It wasn't easy. On my side, it was a struggle. But now I wouldn't trade it for anything.

Survey Says

This question isn't about resolving the substance of a conflict, but about reconnecting after tension or a fight. Some couples have a way of mutually signaling that they have reconnected at some point after tension has occurred, while other couples do not do that. Which best describes you?

	Highly Happy Couples	Mostly Happy Couples	Struggling Couples
We nearly always find a way to purposefully signal or confirm that we have both reconnected. (For example, "Are we okay?" "We're okay." Or a private signal you share with each other that makes sense to the two of you, such as calling each other a pet name, sharing a silly gesture or voice, etc.)	70%	48%	22%
We don't always share a mutual signal that we have reconnected—sometimes we just move on.	30%	52%	78%

Nationally representative and churchgoers' results combined.

Following a time of mutual anger or hurt feelings, if you take the initiative to apologize and "make up" first, does your spouse respond well? (Softening a bit, apologizing in turn, being willing to make up, etc.)

	Highly Happy Couples	Mostly Happy Couples	Struggling Couples
Yes, in those times that I take the initiative first, my spouse generally responds very well—either right then or shortly thereafter.	69%	47%	34%
When I take the initiative first, there's no pattern in my spouse's response—sometimes they respond well; sometimes they don't.	18%	32%	35%
No, in those times when I take the initiative first, my spouse doesn't generally respond in the way I was hoping for.	3%	12%	24%
This doesn't apply, since my spouse is usually the one trying to apologize or make up first	6%	6%	4%
This doesn't apply, since we don't generally resolve things by apologizing or trying to make up.	4%	4%	4%

Note: Due to rounding, some percentages do not total 100%.

Nationally representative and churchgoers' results combined.

Hang Out

How Eliminating Physical Distance Can Solve Emotional Distance

When Jeff and I lived in New York City, our pastor, Tim Keller, preached a sermon one Sunday on friendship. I can still remember one startling fact he shared: Studies showed that the strongest predictor of friendships was not shared values, similar personalities, or a common cultural background. It was proximity.

It turns out that you are most likely to be friends with people you see all the time. Only after that do other factors come into play.

And there's a flip side: even if you have great affinity for each other, if you do *not* live in proximity—and thus simply don't see each other as easily or as often—you're less likely to maintain a close friendship.

A few years later, living in Atlanta, we saw this in action. We were part of a vibrant church small group that met on Thursday nights for fellowship, often dinner. We were always in and out of one another's homes and lives. Then one evening a couple announced they had finally found their dream home. Unfortunately, their new location would mean twenty more minutes of driving time—and they already lived twenty-five minutes away from where we met.

"It won't matter!" we all said to one another. And we were *so* certain. "We'll still be friends! A few miles won't change anything!" We were absolutely determined to stay connected, no matter what.

Do you know what happened? We all tried hard, but the intimacy of the friendship faded. The distance simply beat us. Over time, the now forty-five-minute drive each way proved to be too much. The day came when they sadly shared that they really needed to switch churches to one that was closer to home. We still loved them, still tried to stay up to date. But we lost the closeness we had so enjoyed before.

I'm guessing you have experienced something similar. We get why it happens with friends and neighbors. But what most of us miss is how directly spending time with each other applies to marriage.

I did.

Over and over, the Yes! couples I spoke with mentioned that they do things together. I listened to constant little references to wandering through a Target together on a Saturday, cheering on their kids at sports activities together, enjoying a date night…

Sure, I thought. *Of course they do things together. They're married.*

A couple spending time in each other's company seemed so obvious to me that I completely missed the surprising secret. It took going back over the data from hundreds of interviews before I finally got it. The fact I found is this: *More than 90 percent of the Yes! couples brought up spending time together.* But here's the surprise that almost got away:

Highly happy couples aren't just spending time together because they are happy; a big part of the reason they're so happy is that they are spending time together!

And as you'll see later, there's an important nuance of this secret as well: when these couples are in a season of being at odds with each other—when they are experiencing friction or hurt feelings—they solve it by spending *more* time together instead of less.

How Couple Time Correlates
to "Very Happy"

It turns out, happy couples hang out. Either consciously or subconsciously, they work to maintain their friendship rather than take it for granted. And the most important way they do that is to spend time together. They are in proximity to each other a lot.

Academic studies have confirmed this. As you know from earlier chapters, Dr. Brad Wilcox of the University of Virginia has extensively surveyed married couples, and he gave me some specialized cross-tabulations. In one survey, he asked, "During the past month, about how often did you and your husband/wife spend time alone with each other, talking or sharing an activity?" He found that those married couples who spent *some* sort of time talking or sharing an activity at least once a week *were five times more likely to be "very happy" in their marriages than those who didn't!*[9] (See graph at right or the table at the end of the chapter.)

Do you see the surprising shift in cause and effect? The happiness didn't come first—just sort of drop out of the sky—so *of course* the blissful couple want to be together. Truth is, it happens the other way around. Just as proximity leads to the closest friendships, proximity in marriage leads to the closest couples. The cause is spending quality time together; the effect is happiness.

It turns out that one thing all the Yes! couples have in com-

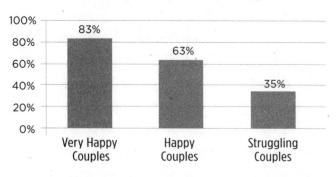

**Percent who hang out
with spouse at least weekly**

mon is that they act as if their marriages are, first and foremost, friendships. And not just any friendship. A happy spouse looks at the other person as their best and closest friend—a friend they want to stay close to no matter what.

> A happy spouse looks at the other
> person as their best and closest friend—
> a friend they want to stay close
> to no matter what.

One husband told me, "For me, getting married was because I wanted a lifelong companion. It wasn't about the sex or the tax write-off. I wanted a built-in best friend for the rest of my life. Most people probably do. So you need to look at the reasons you want to be in the relationship in the first place, and be intentional to make it happen." A Yes! wife gave me a great example:

We went through a season for a few years where things were just hard. We were moving houses, jobs, and schools, and we were at odds on lots of decisions. Instead of being best friends, we were getting on each other's last nerve. Then I realized we were putting more effort into trying to keep our other friendships intact than we were with each other! If I could still get together with my best girlfriend for coffee without letting all the "stuff" get in the way, why couldn't I do that with my husband?

I asked him, "Can we just get together once a week for lunch to catch up on stuff that *isn't* related to which school to choose or the latest problem with the car?" I could see his relief. And that was the beginning of a very different marriage. One where we don't let any *thing* interfere with our friendship.

What Does Quality Time Look Like?

Marriages need quality time, not just quantity time…but it was clear from talking to the Yes! couples that quality time doesn't have to be a romantic dinner over candlelight, sharing deeply in-

timate thoughts and fears. In fact, it usually isn't! Sure, date
nights were often mentioned, but I also heard things like tackling
home projects together, taking evening walks after work, supporting their kids' or grandkids' sports together, prioritizing a
weekend away from the kids, and doing a shared activity—even
if sometimes the shared activity was simply that the wife learned
to enjoy sitting on the couch and watching basketball with her
husband, or that the husband learned to enjoy shopping expedi-
tions (every now and then) to the mall.

> Quality time doesn't have to be a
> romantic dinner over candlelight,
> sharing deeply intimate thoughts and
> fears. In fact, it usually isn't!

One husband who went from a "distant" marriage to a great
marriage told me,

> You know, I looked at the happy couples I knew and I
> realized that they *do* things together. It's not quite the
> same thing as *being* together. It's more purposeful and
> includes the other person in your world. That's different
> from living in the same house but being total strangers.
> I asked my wife what would make her feel like we were

doing something together. I was surprised that it wasn't just the big stuff, like a date night. It turned out that even having coffee together on Saturday mornings, sitting at the same table and reading the newspaper, is something she *loves* because to her it feels like we're connected. We're just hanging out, but we're doing it together, on purpose.

And of course, the Yes! couples tried to simply have fun, and as one wife put it, "Not take things quite so seriously all the time." One wife told me recently, "Our New Year's resolution this year was to stop being fuddy-duddies. We're like 'How did we get to be in our forties but acting like we're stodgy old people?' Instead of being all practical and saying 'No, we don't have time for a vacation' or 'Oh, that would cost a lot,' so what? Go ride a roller coaster or something!"

Friendship by Multiplication

Another vital hanging-out pattern of Yes! couples was that they regularly got together with supportive friends—both peers and mentors who they knew would support their marriages.

Recently, a good friend was struggling with dissatisfaction in her usually happy marriage, and since I was passing through her city, we met for coffee. Her husband had recently taken a pay cut, and she was resenting working many more hours than he was to make up for the shortfall. But as we talked, we found ourselves affirming what a good guy she's married to, how hard he's trying to provide, and how many other wonderful things he does every day that make her feel loved. The next day, my friend left a voice mail:

> I wanted to thank you for your encouragement. I was praying this morning, and God showed me how important it is to hang around the "faith" people. Sometimes I hang around people who are fear based, who say, "You deserve better than this." And it is so crucial to hang out with the people who will build you up, who can see the big picture and keep you encouraged with your spouse instead!

"It is so crucial to hang out with the people who can see the big picture and keep you encouraged with your spouse instead!"

Overcoming Challenges to Together Time

Just like everyone else, highly happy spouses face serious challenges to finding and keeping their hang-out time. But they have found creative ways to be together despite these very real obstacles that could create distance.

1. One or Both Is Unavoidably Gone a Lot

I talked to many Yes! couples who experienced significant separations—for example, he was deployed overseas or she traveled Monday through Thursday for her consulting job. How were they still so happy? Sure, it was hard to be separated, but at least one spouse (if not both) made sure they compensated for the physical absence. I heard solutions like these:

- "We make sure we have date nights or a night out with friends at least once a month, and we arrange a baby-sitter way in advance so we know it's on the calendar."
- "He wants to schedule a phone call most evenings to catch up on the day."
- "Taking late-night flights to get home exhausts me, but I'll sacrifice my body to be back quicker."
- "When he's in town, we make sure we coordinate schedules in advance and let folks know we're going to

miss the baseball game or swim practice because it is 'cave time' for our family."

- "We started having a January annual-planning day to brainstorm what kind of vacation we want to take or what we want to do with the kids each year. We realized we needed to do *something* to get on top of stuff, or otherwise the 'stuff' would take over and we'd never see each other."

Or, as several wives with deployed husbands told me, "Skype is a beautiful thing."

These purposeful attempts to reconnect can't make challenging situations suddenly easy. But they go a long way toward creating the certainty that a husband and wife are best friends, even when they can't have the amount of actual *physical* together time they want.

One husband provided a great word picture: "When we're apart, we are connected by this invisible bungee cord," he told me. "I'm always aware of being pulled toward her."

2. Busyness

Another common challenge to being in proximity is busyness. One wife, who with her husband has mentored dozens of younger couples over the years, put it this way:

A marriage is like a piece of equipment we use and depend on. We have to respect it and treat it well for it to work right and not break. So we respect the marriage and the way it has to work to function properly. But Sol and I often see young married couples who are off in so many different directions, and a part of their busyness—a *big* part of their busyness—doesn't involve their marriage. It's not that you need to do everything with each other, but ultimately a marriage doesn't work right if you're always off doing five different things that have nothing to do with your spouse. You have to be involved, together.

I learned more about overcoming the pull of busyness from another couple I observed arriving at a café at lunchtime one day. She pulled up in one car, and he pulled up in another. Then he came over and began helping her get a baby carrier (complete with baby) out of the backseat. They were both smiling and walking close to each other and, despite the awkwardness of the baby carrier, he reached over and took her hand for the short distance to the café.

Aha! I thought. *That looks like a Yes! couple!*

I used their adorable baby as a conversation starter, then introduced myself and asked if I could ask a few questions. They turned out to be a delightful Kenyan couple who had been living in the United States for a few years. When they said they shared a happy marriage, I asked what kept them happy. They mentioned several different vital factors. Listen in on one:

Him: One thing that keeps us happy is making sure to see each other. Like now, I just took a day off. Just to hang out. I'm in school as well as working, so we don't see each other enough. But we *need* to see each other. Before kids, we used to spend all our time together, but now we have three kids and it's all about them. So we have to try to find time together.

Her: We squeeze time.

Me: You what?

Her: We squeeze time. We squeeze time to be together. The other night, we watched a movie together until one o'clock in the morning. We shouldn't have done it because both of us had work the next day, but we just have to.

Him: Time is the key element. And you have to *make* that time. Because it's not just there—you have to *make* it.

3. Competition from Others for Attention

Parents, in-laws, siblings, friends—even our own kids!—all can be wonderful relationships. But as one happy spouse told me, "Those relationships can also compete for the 'Number One Closest Friend' spot that must be reserved for your spouse alone."

It isn't really surprising that if you are attending to any other relationship more than to the one you share with your spouse, you'll eventually start to feel closer to the other person than you do to your spouse. Strengthening a shaky relationship can often be as simple as refocusing—shifting focus on to a spouse and away from other, lesser priorities.

One stay-at-home mom told me she felt so close to her daughters and so distant from her husband until, as she put it, "I did the math and realized I was spending five hours a day getting the girls ready for school and driving them around and only like fifteen minutes a day with my husband. No wonder I felt closer to them than to him!" With that wake-up call, they made purposeful changes, including his joining her on running their kids to practices, just to cut down their time apart. As she told her daughters, "In eight years, all you kids will be out the door, and your dad and I want to still like each other at that point!"

When God says in Genesis that we should leave our fathers

and mothers (and presumably any other close attachments) and cleave to our spouses, He is not trying to keep us distant from others. Rather, He's telling us to put all other relationships in proper order so that we can ensure that our spouses are our closest friends.

4. A Season of Marital Difficulty

When we have hurt feelings, anger, or discord, the last thing we may want is to be with our spouses. But ultimately, it appears that that is what we most need. I don't mean we should force ourselves to be physically together and keep talking in those moments when we're furious with each other. But during a season of marital discord, spending time together instead of avoiding it actually takes on *more* importance.

Listen to some priceless advice from Joanna Berry, a highly respected marriage counselor and leader with the South Texas Children's Home Ministries, a major regional counseling center:

> With every couple that comes in for marriage counseling, my first question is, "On average in a week, how much time do you spend together as a couple with your attention on each other, without family, kids, TV, and so on, competing for your attention?"

The studies on this have all found the same thing I've seen in my practice. I have never seen a couple who is having problems, who is also having quality time. Never. Instead, they are having problems, so they spend *less* time together in order to avoid the conflict. And then what they think is the solution—avoiding each other— becomes the problem.

Now, obviously, there are a few people who are dealing with huge issues like an alcoholic spouse, and so on, and that's a different situation. But I'm talking about most couples here. And with most couples, how they fell in love was *always* about spending time together. So it makes no sense to get married and stop doing the thing that made you fall in love! *The* common ingredient in attraction and affection is time spent alone together.

I tell these couples, "If you aren't willing to do that quality time together, I can't help you. But if you are, I can."

Berry's homework assignment is often this: she tells them to just be with each other for thirty minutes daily—during which there can be no fighting, no negativity—and to go on a two-hour date night each week. She told me couples return with reports that things are better, but they can't figure out why. She, however, knows exactly why:

> They're finally spending time together again! And this really helps men, especially. He thinks, *Okay, it's not just some vague thing like "be nicer." It's thirty minutes a day. I can do that!* It is such a simple solution. But it really makes a big difference.

"This Is My Beloved and This Is My Friend"

When Jeff and I got married, our theme in the invitations, the favors, and the ceremony itself was a beautiful verse from Song of Solomon 5:16: "This is my beloved and this is my friend." It is fitting that this particular book describes a husband and wife stealing time together, away from the craziness of life.

Most of us probably have had no idea that prioritizing hanging out and doing things together has the power to be such a good protective force around both the love and the friendship in our marriages. But Yes! couples and wise counselors agree.

It really does.

Survey Says

During the past month, about how often did you and your husband/wife spend time alone with each other, talking or sharing an activity?

	Very Happy Couples	Happy Couples	Struggling Couples
At least weekly.	83%	63%	35%
Less than weekly.	17%	37%	65%

Source: Dr. Brad Wilcox, *Survey of Marital Generosity, 2010–2011*.

Don't Tell It Like It Is

What Happens When You Give Brutal Honesty the Boot

Samantha is one of the funniest women I've ever met. She has a way of blurting out what everyone else is thinking but isn't brave enough to say. At parties, Samantha's clever disclosures and sharp wit routinely leave friends gasping with laughter. And sometimes…wincing slightly.

Unfortunately, Samantha (not her real name) is facing challenges in her marriage. She told me not long ago, "Our counselor told us we needed to be more open with each other."

We both laughed. *Samantha, more open! How?*

But as she went on, I began to sense a problem. Describing a conversation she'd had with her husband the previous night, she said she had chewed him out for letting the kids "play him for a sucker." She said she told him to "get a clue."

When I reflexively grimaced, she put her hands on her hips and stared at me. "What?" she challenged, eyebrows raised. "In marriage, we should be able to be brutally honest with each other! I tell him what I think; he tells me what he thinks. We don't pull any punches. This is who I am, and I don't think I should have to change."

Suddenly, I had a pretty good idea why their marriage was in trouble.

My mind jumped back to something a happily married man had remarked on the day before. "Some people have this weird dedication to being ultradirect, not caring how it's perceived," he told me. "They say, 'Hey, that's just the way I am—take it or leave it.' Well, yeah, that may be the way you are, but that is why you're being left! How's that working for you?"

Is it possible that what works at a party doesn't work in marriage—at least not so well, and maybe not at all?

In this chapter we're going to look at the way words can build or destroy, seem okay in one situation but not another, make you happy but maybe make your spouse miserable. At its heart, this chapter is about the power of kindness.

Let's start with Samantha's strong feelings about the virtues of being brutally honest.

The Genius of Pulling Punches

You hear those two words—*brutally honest*—together all the time these days. People have said it to me for years in my interviews. They say what you'd expect—that being brutally honest with each other is important in a relationship. "You have to put it out there, make sure you're calling it exactly like you see it, not pull any punches." But let me share a most surprising discovery: *I never heard a single Yes! couple use those words.*

Once I had made this observation, I became more intentional about verifying it. Then, when I met a woman who was blessed with a very happy marriage *and* a cleverly sarcastic sense of humor, I saw my opportunity. What was the role of brutal honesty in her marriage? I asked. Any insights she could share?

"Brutal honesty?" she repeated, showing some alarm. "No, no, no!" she said. "Sure, in marriage you absolutely need to be able to share things that make you want to jump out a window. I need to, anyway. I need to know I can go deep with him. But that's also *when I have to be the most careful to not hurt him.*"

The more data I gathered, the more obvious this secret became:

💡 Highly happy couples treat one another with intentional
   kindness; they joke and they challenge, but they try
   to never do it in ways their mate would perceive as
   disrespectful or hurtful.

You can see the telling results from the survey at the end of
the chapter. In one question, I asked the survey takers to evaluate
how much consideration their mates show when they are alone
together—and learned that highly happy couples weren't just
putting on a show. Behind closed doors they put in just as much
effort to be considerate with their spouses as they did with friends
in public. Fully 71 percent of the Yes! spouses said their mate usually puts in as much or *more* effort into being considerate with
them in private as they did while on their best behavior in public.
But only 55 percent of mostly happy and just 28 percent of struggling spouses agreed.

But then the second question pointed directly at the person
taking the survey and asked, essentially, "Okay, then—how are
you doing at being considerate, yourself?"

Interestingly, most survey takers' assessment of themselves
wasn't that far off from what their spouse believed about them.
Fully 75 percent of highly happy spouses tried to be just as considerate in private, where only 46 percent of struggling spouses did.

(See graph.) The one exception was that far more struggling spouses thought they were being considerate; so either they are deluded (always a possibility), trying hard but not succeeding (also a possibility), or their spouses simply weren't giving their efforts enough credit.

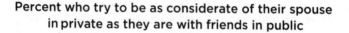

Percent who try to be as considerate of their spouse in private as they are with friends in public

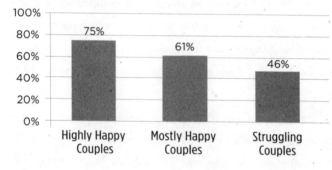

In any case, the struggling relationships are lacking in perceived or actual kindness. Neither spouse feels like their mate is a supportive, safe haven in a stressful, harsh world.

By contrast, one reason the highly happy couples are so happy is that they value kindness rather than telling it like it is. Instead of letting their conversations be seasoned with brutal honesty, these couples choose to follow the apostle Paul's advice to the church in the ancient city of Colossae—to "let your conversation be always full of grace." They understand the power of words to destroy and that nowhere is this power to be more in control than in the relationships that matter to us most.

Would You Say That to a Friend?

Sometimes when I share these findings at speaking events, people look concerned. One woman asked, "But shouldn't we be *able* to let our guard down with our spouses and *not* be on our best behavior? Should we have to walk on eggshells? Isn't marriage supposed to be the one safe place we can be ourselves and not be so 'on' all the time?"

Yes, of course! But treating your spouse with kindness is not the same thing as walking on eggshells. And as one person put it, "You should be able to let your guard down. You should be able to be relaxed and safe. You should be able to make mistakes and have your spouse forgive you. But that doesn't mean it's okay to have a pattern of treating your spouse poorly."

Several others have asked whether I'm suggesting that we censor ourselves instead of being honest. Not at all. Over and over, I heard things like this comment from one happy husband: "So often *it's not just what you say but how you say it* that matters. I was on the subway this morning, listening to this lady talking to her husband. There was this derisive tone. She was almost rolling her eyes at him. And I thought, *Would you* ever *have said those things to a close friend? Or even a casual acquaintance? If not, why would you ever say that to the person you're supposed to love the most?* She could have asked exactly the same types of questions, but if they were in a tone of 'help me understand,' it would have felt like she actually cared about him."

Often, in fact, that was the line the Yes! couples advised others never to cross: *if you wouldn't say it that way to a close friend, don't say it that way to your spouse.*

> The line the Yes! couples advised others never to cross: if you wouldn't say it that way to a close friend, don't say it that way to your spouse.

Different Cultures, Different Expressions... Same Need for Care

One of the hardest things for me to figure out was the role of cultural differences in how couples approached this issue of openness and candor. For example, I interviewed many Yes! couples where one or both spouses were black or Latino, and most of them said that they viewed their cultures as more vocal or demonstrative than other ethnic groups. And because of that, I began to see that one of my early hypotheses—that Yes! couples don't have as much emotional conflict—was simply not universal. Instead, kindness and caring for the other person's feelings were what was universal.

As one wife told me, "Yeah, he can get on my last nerve sometimes, and I tell him so. But getting in someone's face sometimes isn't the same thing as being unkind. I can be vocal and still be careful of his feelings. It is a matter of understanding where *he* draws the line."

I was interviewing one pastor, who shared, "I went to a mostly white Bible college and a friend asked, 'Why are black people mad at each other all the time?' I told him, 'We're not mad; we're expressive.' Being expressive and having a 'tone'…does that transfer to marriage? Yes. We're just like that. But does that mean we should *ever* treat others better than our spouses? No, that is not the case."

His wife nodded. "I would use that tone and that conflict with a girlfriend too. But the problem comes when we start hurting the other person and don't care. That is definitely a heart issue."

The pastor continued, "Culturally, things are expressed differently. The expression of displeasure may be more demonstrative and passionate, yes. But disrespect is disrespect. And I cannot think that a happily married couple would ever be okay with that."

It is worth noting that this cultural distinction was not universal; although about half of the African American and Latino Yes! couples I interviewed said that they believed they could be more expressive and still be kind, the other half disagreed.

As one such wife commented, "I want him to hear what I have to say. And if I can't talk to him right, at the right time, it will be more of a hassle. So I've learned how to be quiet and patient and wait for my time. Timing is everything. And it is also my tone when I talk to him. Sometimes, I can be really mad. I've learned if I can say it in a softer tone, he can hear it."

Her husband nodded. "That is so true. She is *not* a nag. And she's figured out how to say it. Like, when she's upset that I'm butting heads with the kids, and her tone is 'I'm correcting you because you're wrong,' then I shut down. But when she is more exploratory and says 'Do you know your son feels like this and that you came across this way?' it is easier for me to listen. She is clearly just trying to have a conversation. I don't feel offended and like I have to disagree with her just to make my point."

What *Safe* Is Not

Ironically, some say the reason they treat their spouses more roughly than they do friends is that their marriages are safe places. But all my research indicates that rough treatment, including taking advantage of where a spouse is weak, strips away the very safety they want to take advantage of. One happy wife gave me a great illustration:

> It is so important to not take advantage of the other's weaknesses. For example, I am not a good fighter. In fact, I hate fighting. I hate any negative vibes and avoid it at all costs. And Darren knows it, but he doesn't mind fighting and he's a great debater. So in a verbal disagreement, he owns me. And once or twice early on, he'd almost bully me verbally. He naturally sensed weakness and went in for the kill. Not to hurt me so much as to win the debate. I would wind up crying, and he felt awful.
>
> So one day, he came over to where I was crying and hugged me and said, "Never again… I will never take advantage of that again." And he hasn't. In fact, he knows I will avoid telling him why I'm mad, to avoid conflict. So now he purposefully drags it out of me because he genuinely wants to improve our marriage and not make me feel that way again. Wow. If you think about it, that must take so much discipline and love, to sit there and ask me to say all these negative things. And to be kind and not use my weakness against me. It is totally selfless,

and it shows that he's fully vested in our marriage. That one thing, more than any other, genuinely blows me away.

But how do you manage to create that kind of selfless, safe place in your marriage? A delightful couple I met and interviewed on the road shared something very important:

Her: Marcus always talks positively about me. It's so good to feel safe and know I won't get put down— even if he's lying through his teeth when he says I look beautiful in the morning! When someone speaks positively to you, it makes you more positive toward the other person.

Me: Marcus, how can you do that every day? Surely there are days that you don't feel like it?

Him: My first thoughts may be selfish sometimes! But, well…for me it is about following what God says in the Bible. My first thoughts may otherwise be selfish, but I'm instructed to love her as Christ loves her. If I'm truly listening to God, regardless of the emotion I feel, I'll be all those things.

Her: You do listen. And that makes me feel secure.

Can you say "Aww" on cue?

What I noticed in all my conversations with highly happy couples was that they were enjoying the very intimacy that some struggling couples thought could only come through brutal honesty.

What the T-Shirt Said

I was out grocery shopping one day when I saw this perfect quote on the back of someone's T-shirt:

Be kind, for everyone you meet is fighting a great battle.
—Philo of Alexandria[10]

I will confess that I almost knocked over a stack of produce as I hurried to get close enough to write it down.

Everyone is made in wonderfully different ways—from my snappy friend Samantha to the "aww" couple I quoted above. Living out this particular secret of happy couples doesn't mean taking on any particular personality. But it does mean being kind.

And if you think about it, since you would never want to signal to a close friend that "I can treat you any way I want, and you'll still be my friend," why would you do that with your spouse who is supposed to be your closest friend in the world? So give your spouse permission to (kindly!) point out ways you might in fact be doing that but you just hadn't seen. At the same time, find ways to show kindness regularly.

You and your spouse will hopefully find that although you may be "fighting a great battle" out there in the world every day, you are fighting it safely, kindly…and together.

Survey Says

When most of us are with friends or acquaintances, we put forward effort to be on our best behavior. When you are alone with your spouse, do you think your spouse puts in as much effort to be considerate with you as he or she does in public with other people?

	Highly Happy Couples	Mostly Happy Couples	Struggling Couples
Yes, my spouse puts in more effort than he/she does with others.	34%	20%	14%
Yes, my spouse puts in a similar effort as with others.	37%	35%	14%
Sometimes yes; sometimes no.	26%	37%	49%
Not really; my spouse generally puts in less effort than with others.	4%	9%	23%

Note: Due to rounding, some percentages do not total 100%.

When you are alone with your spouse, do you generally put in the same effort to be considerate of your spouse as you do with others?

	Highly Happy Couples	Mostly Happy Couples	Struggling Couples
Yes, I make even more effort to treat my spouse well than I do with others.	45%	22%	21%
Yes, I make the same type of effort with my spouse as I do with others.	30%	39%	25%
Sometimes I do that; sometimes I don't.	20%	29%	47%
Not really; I let my guard down with my spouse, so I just don't think about it.	6%	10%	7%

Note: Due to rounding, some percentages do not total 100%.

Highly Happy Couples

Look Higher

Why Looking to Marriage
for Happiness Means You're
Looking in the Wrong Place

A few years back when I was interviewing young people for *For Parents Only,* I stumbled on something I didn't quite expect. The happiest kids weren't those whose parents prioritized the kids above everything else, making their whole lives revolve around them. Instead, the happiest kids seemed to be those who knew their parents loved and cared for them but who could tell that Mom and Dad prioritized the family unit and their marriage even more. Even the most independent-minded teens felt more secure when they knew their parents were looking higher than at whatever their children wanted at that moment.

Secretly, children were a lot happier when they knew that someone older and wiser was in charge.

In this current project, I have been finding a fascinating parallel among the happiest couples. You might think that the happiest spouses placed their marriages or each other above everything else. But—counterintuitive as it might seem—that often was not the case at all. They, too, looked higher—ordering their homes and relationships around a transcendent priority. And as a result they, too, were more secure and happy.

What Could Matter More than the Marriage?

Listen in on a representative conversation with one happy couple, married forty-three years, that I interviewed after interrupting them as they shared hot dogs at an airport:

Me: If people ask "What's your secret?" what do you tell them?

Him: Put her first, and hug her.

Me: Aww, that is sweet.

Her: Well, actually…I know he'll agree with this too, but that's not the real secret. The real secret is

Jesus Christ. Putting Him at the center of our
marriage.

Him: Yes, it really is. He gives us the ability to love each
other, put each other first, and stick with it, even
when we haven't wanted to.

Even though I interviewed hundreds of people outside of
church-related venues—many of whom, statistically speaking, I
expected to *not* believe in God—the randomly encountered happy
couples I spoke to kept bringing Him up. It didn't matter whether
I was in an urban subway station in Newark or an upscale coffee
shop in Omaha; whether I was talking to an elderly white pair or
a young African American couple. Although it didn't happen
with everyone, more often than not, the happiest spouses mentioned that faith in God was vitally important to their marriages.

> The happiest spouses often
> mentioned that faith in God was
> vitally important to their marriages.

Relying on Him gave them the security of knowing that
Someone higher than themselves was in control—Someone on
whom they each could rely on for the selflessness needed to put the
other person first and create a great marriage. Not only that, but

the knowledge that their spouses were looking to God for fulfillment—rather than to them—took the pressure off trying to provide something that, in the end, only God can really provide.

Now, I know that not all readers will relate to the spirituality many couples mentioned. If that is the case for you, please don't feel excluded. After all, many couples I interviewed who *weren't* people of faith were also wonderfully happy. Still, in this one chapter we will address issues of faith directly. Many demographers and sociologists have found that those who share a belief in God and regularly worship together are statistically more likely to be happy in their marriages, and that trend was apparent in my research as well.[11]

And that fact is also foundational for the secret we will be covering in this chapter:

Highly happy couples tend to put God at the center of their marriage and focus on Him, rather than on their marriage or spouse, for fulfillment and happiness.

They Look Higher

I saw that God-centered happiness repeatedly in my interviews, but quantifying it required more specialized data. Again, I turned to the data Dr. Brad Wilcox provided me. It turns out that couples in which both partners agree that "God is at the center of our marriage" are twice as likely to report that they are very happy than those who do not agree. (See graph below and the Survey Says section.) Many other studies have found similar trends.[12]

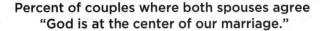

Percent of couples where both spouses agree "God is at the center of our marriage."

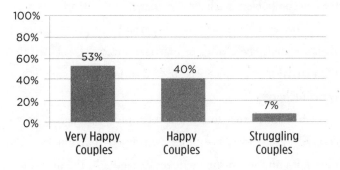

Again, although many Yes! couples did not share a faith commitment, centering a marriage on God first and foremost is clearly one huge success factor for a happy marriage. And one habit that sets many Yes! couples apart is *not* looking to their spouses as their primary source of happiness. Instead, they look higher.

Let's examine how this habit plays out in the lives of Yes! couples.

What Looking Higher Looks Like

1. They Worship Together

Overwhelmingly, those Yes! couples who brought up reliance on God said they attended church together. Instead of a *belief* in God being the key factor, the commitment to do something about it—starting with going to church together—seems to be the key component in a happy marriage.

"Now wait," you may say. "I've heard that going to church *doesn't* change the chance of marriage success. I've heard that the marriages of churchgoers succeed or fail at the same rate as nonchurchgoers!"

I had heard that too, but it isn't true. Although there are certainly exceptions, the more committed individuals are to their faith and to worshiping together regularly, the more likely they are to have a marriage that lasts and to be happy in that marriage.

The notion that that isn't the case is based on a misunderstanding of Barna Group studies from the last few decades—studies that analyzed the rate of marriage survival or divorce based on *religious beliefs* rather than *actions* like church attendance. For my book *The Good News About Marriage* (releasing soon after this one), I partnered with the Barna Group to do a new analysis of their data that included church attendance. I found that the marriages of those who attend church weekly are far more likely to survive. Their divorce rate drops by at least 27 percent compared to those who do not. Other in-depth studies have found an average drop of around 50 percent.[13]

2. They Are Plugged Into a Faith Community

As noted in chapter 9, one very clear habit of the Yes! couples was a mutual friendship with other positive, supportive couples, including mentors. So it makes sense that churchgoing Yes! couples were highly likely to mention the need not just to go to church but also to be plugged in and active in their faith community. These couples mentioned being in home groups together, doing group Bible studies, engaging in service projects together, and so on—all of which are venues that provide opportunities to befriend, get support from, and share life with others.

3. They Share Key Values

Although I certainly spoke to some Yes! couples where the two partners identified with two different faiths, I found that to be a less common situation. One of the reasons that many committed churchgoing Yes! couples were happy is that both spouses were trying to adhere to a higher, external standard (the Bible) that they both agreed on, and thus they weren't as likely to have a severe clash of values about important life topics such as parenting, sex, and money.

That's not to say they didn't have those clashes at all or that they always agreed. (Any churchgoer reading this knows *that's* not true!) Still, shared values—especially if both spouses believed those values were rooted in a higher law—dramatically reduced the opportunities for serious conflict.

4. They Focus on Serving Their Spouses, Rather Than on Being Served

The importance of a focus on serving rather than being served received multiple mentions regardless of whether or not the person I was talking to was a person of faith. But the vast majority of Christian couples I interviewed brought it up. As one husband put it,

> I really feel like the church has to do a better job of teaching its people what God created marriage to be.
>
> The problem is, when you decide to get married, it's because this person is meeting your needs. There's something about this person and how they treat you. They make you feel special or loved or appreciated, and

that feels so good and right. But when we stand at the altar, we promise to meet *their* needs—regardless! We need to realize that that is how God created marriage to work. Because if we don't make that switch, there may come a day when we think, *Hey! My needs aren't being met… There's no reason to be married!*

One amazing couple I know has mentored many dozens of couples over the years. The husband mentioned a young engaged couple whom he felt would "be just fine." When I asked why, he explained, "After discussing things over the last few weeks, Evan met me for coffee yesterday and said, 'I now realize that I'm asking Mariah for the privilege of serving her for the rest of her life, not for getting my needs met for the rest of my life.'"

> "I now realize that I'm asking Mariah for the privilege of serving her for the rest of her life, not for getting my needs met for the rest of my life."

He thought for a moment, then continued, "And that shift is what is likely to make *both* of them happy for the rest of their lives. Nothing is certain, you know. But it is a lot more likely."

5. They Look to God for That Power to Be Selfless— Because It Doesn't Come Naturally!

I don't know about you, but I realize I've got a lot of selfishness I don't want to admit to. And I come face to face with it in marriage. It shows up in the littlest things—like when my husband excitedly wants to show me his latest idea for his business and I really want to keep drinking my morning coffee, thank you very much. It makes me wonder—if that is how I feel sometimes on the *little* things, how can I ever expect to be selfless on the big ones?

I'm not alone. The Yes! couples mentioned the same deep-down struggle. But they also frequently mentioned the answer—and it wasn't simple willpower. Because if selfishness is indeed (as the Bible says) deep down in our natures, it would be pretty hard to generate enough willpower to consistently do the selfless, loving, giving thing. Every. Single. Time.

Now, obviously, none of us can truly be perfectly selfless! But the Bible does give hope that a higher power is available to help. For example, in one of his letters, the apostle Paul wrote, "See that no one pays back evil for evil, but always try to do good to each other and to everyone else." He then promises, "God will make this happen, for he who calls you is faithful."

I'm sure that is why many of the Yes! couples (including some I didn't know were people of faith when we started talking) emphasized the need to rely on God's power—not our own. As I heard Atlanta pastor Leonce Crump put it recently, "Positive thinking does not change your heart. It is only Christ who can push out your poison and pull in new life."[14]

6. Ultimately, They Trust God for the Outcome

I have spoken to enough couples on both ends of the happiness spectrum to know that it can be scary to commit to meeting your spouse's needs regardless of whether you expect to get your own needs met.

But a powerful paradox can be hiding in that exchange. In fact, trusting God instead of another to meet your needs might be the most enduring security-producing choice you ever make.* As one happy wife put it,

> It is a risk to open yourself to the other person, but ultimately it's safe because the One you are ultimately trusting and putting your life in the hands of is *God,* not your spouse. After all, in the end there is no human

---

* We recognize that in a small percentage of marriages, such as with a spouse that is physically abusive, trusting God may lead to a very different outcome. If you are in that situation, we urge you to remember that this book is designed for the average couples who make up the vast majority of marriages, not those who are experiencing serious problems such as abuse, and we urge you to reach out to a trusted counselor or pastor to get the help you need.

relationship you can ever trust 100 percent not to hurt you, because that other person isn't God! But you can trust God 100 percent.

Yes, it is so important to give yourself over to your spouse fully. To eliminate all walls and invest fully. To believe with all your heart that your spouse wants to and will become the person you need. To believe they will never betray you. All that. But don't put your spouse on a pedestal and look to them or put your faith in them to make you happy. That is God's job. You and your spouse together need to trust each other, submit to each other, and lean on God together.

How About Door Number Three?

Ultimately, it was clear that looking higher allowed the happiest marriages to flourish because each partner was looking to God for fulfillment and security and was *not* looking to marriage for something it was not designed to deliver. A large number of Yes! couples emphasized that although it is wonderful to want and to work for happy marriages, expecting marriage (or our spouses) to make us happy is a trap, since there is no human relationship that holds the key to happiness. Only God can provide that ultimate fulfillment we are all longing for.

As I studied the Yes! couples and listened to them talk about this, I realized that their example holds the answer to a question that has been debated often in the Christian community: How should we think and talk about happiness in marriage? As the book *Sacred Marriage* memorably asks, what if God designed marriage to make us holy more than to make us happy? Given the corrosive cultural trend toward "If I'm not happy, I'm out of here," pastors and Christian leaders often wonder whether we should take the desire for happiness off the table and focus exclusively on the (very real) need for marital selflessness and sacrifice.

But I think that the Yes! couples show us that we don't have to choose between the two.

A few years ago, Paul and Virginia Friesen, the directors of Home Improvement Ministries, a marriage and family ministry near Boston, invited Jeff and me to conduct a weekend marriage conference. During a break, we all began discussing whether the holiness-or-happiness question implies that the two are mutually exclusive. Paul nearly jumped out of his chair because this hit such a nerve with him. He said,

> Nearly every day in counseling, I see troubled couples who have come to believe that they have two choices. They believe they can either stay together and be miserable, or split up and be happy.

I say, "How about door number three? Stay together and be happy!" People need to believe that that is possible.

Working toward and believing in an abundant, strong, happy marriage is not the same thing as looking to marriage to make you happy. But that desire for a wonderful marriage certainly seems to be God given and something we should celebrate, because people need hope. Not hope *outside* their marriages—but hope for happiness *in* their marriages!

And thankfully, although in this fallen world there are no guarantees, it is clearly true that the habit of putting God first and serving the other person will usually make you happier in the end. This is what God seems to have intended.

I'll conclude with the words of one Yes! couple who had gone from having a pattern of hurt feelings, explosions, and bitterness to having a great marriage. They stumbled into many of the habits in this book as part of their journey to get there. But they shared that for them the most life-changing part was treating each other the way God commands—not just to please the other, but to please God first. As the husband shared,

We got on same page and realized we had to be pleasing to God. Our main goal now is to make sure we're pleasing

Him, and we reap the benefits. If I treat you the way God wants me to, then you'll be happy. And then I'll be happy. Wow—that's a great deal!

Survey Says

Please indicate how much you agree or disagree with the following statement: "God is at the center of our marriage."

	Very Happy Couples	Happy Couples	Struggling Couples
Both agree ("Somewhat" to "Strongly").	53%	40%	7%
Both disagree ("Somewhat" to "Strongly").	26%	44%	30%
One spouse agrees; one disagrees.	30%	44%	26%

Source: Dr. Brad Wilcox, *Survey of Marital Generosity, 2010–2011.*

Get In over Their Heads

Why Risking It All on Your
Marriage Is Actually the Safest Bet

Take a minute to join me in this imaginary scenario. You're
back in high school, you have several groups of friends, the
weekend is coming up, and you'll do what you always do—manage your social calendar on the fly, thanks to your smartphone.

(If you're old enough to be thinking *But I didn't have a smartphone in high school,* just work with me here.)

Thursday in the cafeteria your friend Tami says, "Hey, come
over tomorrow and let's hang out. I'm baby-sitting my little sister.
But we could watch a movie or something."

Now you face a classic conundrum of Teenlandia: you can accept Tami's invitation immediately, or you can wait to see if a more exciting option comes along.

Here's what you do: You hedge your bets. Even though you like Tami just fine, you say, "Sounds…great. Listen, I'll get back to you." In the meantime you watch your phone to see what else pops up.

By Friday afternoon, you realize to your dismay that *nothing* else is going to pop up. Have your other friends forgotten you exist? Does the world suddenly hate you? (Remember, you're in high school.) After school, you run into Tami.

"Well?" she says. "You coming or not?"

Time to decide. "Yeah, sure!" you chirp. "I'll be there. Thanks!"

Friday night finds you on the couch with Tami. You tell her you're having fun. But the truth? You're *still* hedging your bets. See, you brought money for a late movie just in case somebody calls. Every time Tami's not looking, you pull out your phone to keep the lines open with your other friends. You send Marc a smiley face. You poke Kyra on Facebook. You text a "What you doin'?" to Megan—and you don't even like her very much.

Here's a question: in this imaginary scenario, how much do

you think you will enjoy your evening with Tami? Speaking for myself as a teen, I would have had a wasted evening. My restlessness and dissatisfaction would have stolen the simple joy of hanging out with a friend.

But now I want you to reimagine that Friday evening, adding a slight twist: When you finally say yes to Tami, you go all in. You put all other possibilities for your upcoming evening *out of your mind*. When Kyra does in fact text you to ask if you want to go to a movie with her, Marc, and Megan, you quickly reply, "Would've loved to, but I'm helping Tami baby-sit. Catch you tomorrow."

Now ask yourself, *How might my evening have unfolded then? All else being equal, wouldn't I have enjoyed it a whole lot more?*

This chapter is about a critical choice that shapes every relationship. That choice is like a toggle switch: Flip it one way and you're somewhat committed. Flip it the other and you're all in.

I'll admit that the choice to be all in when it comes to marriage isn't always popular these days. And there are many ways people don't even realize that they aren't fully committed. But the simple truth is, how you throw that switch—and being aware of the choice—radically determines the quality of your marriage.

And the happiest couples I've met are happy in large part because they take the risk to go all in.

Highly Happy Couples Enjoy "Unprotected" Love

My research clearly shows that the happiest couples consistently risk everything to commit. That commitment showed up in relational, emotional, and even financial ways. And the risks were real: they chose to willingly put themselves at risk of getting their hearts broken, looking like fools, or experiencing the debilitating pain of betrayal.

Put simply, the Yes! couples didn't hedge their bets. They didn't try to wall off a piece of themselves "just in case." Here's the secret:

💡 Highly happy couples take the risk of getting their hearts broken or looking like fools, they fully invest emotionally instead of holding back to protect themselves, and because they are all in, they have dramatically increased security and happiness.

On the combined survey, while more than half of all struggling couples felt it was important to maintain a bit of emotional independence, 72 percent of Yes! couples said the opposite! (See graph at right.)

Percent of spouses who try *not* to protect themselves emotionally

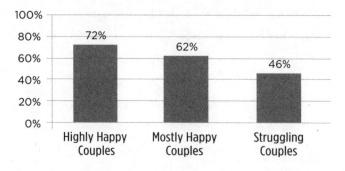

The feeling of maintaining emotional independence or protecting oneself on the inside can reveal itself in different ways on the outside. As just one of hundreds of examples, a wife who is protecting herself a bit isn't likely to share her innermost thoughts with her husband. Maybe she's worried he might laugh at her. So she might share some things with her girlfriends that she wouldn't with her husband.

Similarly, a man who wants to maintain emotional independence might defend his twice-a-week poker night with the guys, no matter what's happening at home. Or he might pour himself into his work as an excuse to not be fully involved with his wife.

Of course, having guy friends and girlfriends to hang out with is a blessing. Yes! couples do that too. But there's an important difference. Yes! couples do not use outside commitments, people, and interests as a retreat from their marriages. They actively veer away from any Teenlandia "just in case" strategies.

And they hold nothing back—even in areas as critical and potentially scary as how they manage their money.

> Highly happy couples hold nothing back—even in areas as critical and potentially scary as how they handle money.

The Missing Stash of Cash

What does being all in actually look like in real life? This is where it gets surprising. Dozens of Yes! spouses told me that unlike some of their friends, they had no secret personal bank accounts. Often against the counsel of others—and often in spite of their own instincts—they took the risk to be fully trusting and open, with no hidden means of support if it all went south.

One Yes! wife captured the significance of her choice:

You could say, "Well, that is foolish today. You have to be prudent." But what is more foolish? Taking the risk to trust him and risking the small likelihood that your spouse will betray you? Or deciding that you're *not* going to fully trust him and risking the almost *certain* likelihood that it will build a wall between you and undermine your marriage?

In her view, the act of hiding something on the side would actually *invite* a divided and undermined marriage. Where's the security in that? Highly happy couples didn't enter lightly into their choice to be all in—in many cases, they were choosing to do the opposite of what they had been taught or what others advised. And the outcome for many has been dramatic. For example, for this couple:

> **Her:** My dad encouraged us girls to hold a little something back. He'd say, "You've got to go out and get a job so you don't have to depend on a man." And my mom implanted that idea too. When we got married, she'd tell us to put some of each paycheck aside somewhere he couldn't get to it. She always had her stash and my dad knew it. When I got married, in the back of my mind, I thought, *If bad stuff ever happens, I have to have my own separate account in place.*
>
> **Me:** What is the consequence of that?
>
> **Him:** One word. *Death.*

Her: It creates a wedge. There is intimacy not shared. There's a missing link, a missing trust that creates that wedge. If you can't be vulnerable enough to trust your spouse in that area, then there's going to be weakness in other areas of your relationship. Because there can't be this fear and suspicion— and really, that's what it is. You have to be able to relinquish that and trust each other. If you can't, then there's a bigger issue that hasn't been resolved. When I got serious about my walk with Christ, I eventually realized that I have to trust God and trust my husband.

Him: I work in a big call center, answering phones, and every year, the VP comes down to tell us the year-end bonus money we made. And every year he says, "You know the credit union—that's a good place to hide money from your wife." He says, "If I don't hide it, she's going to spend it all." But if there's a part of your life you refuse to share, you never truly go to that point where you become one. If you can't trust the person, it's going to be difficult in so many other areas. So when she finally decided to trust me—trust God *and* me, I guess— that's when everything changed.

So How to Get from Here to All In

You might be wondering how couples move in their relationship from mostly in to all in. Is it a one-time leap of faith? Or are there certain beliefs and attitudes that make it, while still risky, the most sensible choice a loving couple can make?

My research turned up four important core beliefs and actions that make all the difference for highly happy marriages. I've framed them here as first-person declarations because that's how I most often heard these husbands and wives say them—with complete finality and confidence.

1. "I Assume That Having a Happy Marriage Is Not Just Possible but Likely"

Nearly without exception, the happiest couples told me they had survived difficult times by believing that a happy marriage was not only possible but also likely for them. And that belief seems to create a huge psychological advantage. Look at this comment from a woman who has gone through fire in her marriage and come out the other side:

> You can't listen to [the naysayers]. Instead, you need to assume your marriage *will* last. One of the thoughts that helped me to make it through my first pregnancy, fighting

the fear of the coming pain that everyone tells you is the worst pain ever, was the thought that millions and millions of women over the centuries have successfully given birth, *So I can do this too!*

It is the same principle in considering making one's marriage last. I think, If so many others have succeeded, *I'll keep trying and I will probably also succeed!*

There is great skepticism in our culture about marriage today. It leads to a sense of futility that can be insidiously fatal to a marriage encountering difficulty, since one or both spouses begin to subconsciously think, *Why bother trying if we're just going to be one of the statistics in the end?* But Yes! couples will have none of it. As one happy husband put it, "The belief that a lifelong, great marriage is impossible is self-fulfilling. And your cynicism prevents the very thing you want but are cynical about! You have to assume your marriage will be just fine."

Fortunately, such apparently pie-in-the-sky confidence is based on solid data. In fact, there is far more good news about marriage than we realize. I already mentioned the good news about the strength of marriage for churchgoers in the last chapter, but there's more. I lay out even more (and surprising) facts in my book *The Good News About Marriage*—but a quick overview can provide a starting point.[15]

For example, a commonly accepted belief these days is that half of all marriages end in divorce. That's not even *close* to true!

First, according to 2009 US Census Bureau data, 72 percent of people are still married to their first spouse. Yes, you read that right! And even when second and third marriages are included, the current prevalence of divorce among the general population is somewhere around 30 percent! That is still too high, of course, but knowing that roughly 70 percent of all marriages are surviving is much more hopeful than the myth suggests.

> Contrary to popular opinion, the vast majority of marriages are happy, with the couple enjoying being married—not just putting up with each other!

But there's more. Contrary to popular opinion, the vast majority of marriages are happy, with the couple *enjoying* being married—not just putting up with each other! When I have asked people, "What percentage of marriages do you think are happy?" they usually guess "about 30 percent." But the real average is around 80 percent! Or more! Although most marriages encounter inevitable difficulties—some fleeting, some substantial—the vast majority of couples still describe their unions as happy ones.

All this is *very* good news—and helps to make the case for

being all in, in your marriage. The "We can do this!" attitude of happy couples is based on both choice *and* fact.

2. "We Never Use the D-Word, Because Divorce Isn't an Option"

There's a scripture that says, "As far as it depends on you, live at peace with everyone" (Romans 12:18). The Yes! spouses worked hard to apply this advice in many ways—but one very specific and almost universal method was to adhere to the rule that, as one wife put it, "As far as it depends on you, never use the D-word."

As one husband summarized, "Divorce is not ever an option. No reason to mention or consider it. So I love how that will pressure us to find a solution."

And even if it had been considered before, I've seen some amazing things happen when a couple starts over with the commitment to never discuss it again. I spoke to one woman who said she realized she introduced "death" to her marriage by saying things like "Well, maybe we should just get divorced" or "Fine, divorce me, then" when she was upset. So she went to her husband and apologized and told him she would never do that again.

"That is not going to be an option for us," she told me. "We still have other problems to work through, but I know we're going to beat them. He told me that the one thing I did that made the biggest difference was when I stopped throwing the D-word out there in the heat of the moment. Taking that off the table actually changes how we feel about each other because we're on the same team again—permanently."

Taking away the divorce option also eliminates that dangerous sense of futility. All-in couples, I discovered, can experience bad months, bad years, plenty of insecurity…but no sense of futility. Why? Because they know they will be married for the rest of their lives, regardless.

Believing that they will succeed is a self-fulfilling prophecy.

Of course, all this said, we can only control what *we* do, not what our spouses do. Several of my close girlfriends are now divorced because they were abandoned by their husbands; one close relative was abandoned by his wife. There just are cases where one spouse has no say in the ultimate outcome. But even if your spouse *does* throw the D-word around, you can resolve that, as far as it depends on you, you never will. And I've heard from several couples that this stance is catching.

The Yes! couples who had gone through the fire and out the other side said that knowing that they would be married no matter what was a powerful incentive to figure out how to make that a good thing rather than a bad thing. As one wife put it,

We went through some tough times because both of us come from broken homes, single moms, with siblings all by different fathers. But our commitment made the difference. Divorce was never an option, but I didn't want to be miserable either, so we had to say, "Let's figure out how this works."

Today, we are one of the couples who mentor folks through premarital counseling at our church. We tell them that knowing marriage is forever doesn't mean you won't have arguments. But it means you have a much better chance of navigating through those arguments and coming out on top. When you put God at the head of your marriage and know that He says marriage is forever, the only option is "Let's work through it."

We've been doing this premarital counseling for years now, and what we've seen is that in the end, it didn't matter what their backgrounds were; it mattered how determined they were to have a good marriage.

> "When marriage is forever, the only option is 'Let's work through it.'"

3. "I Believe My Spouse Is There for Me and Isn't Going to Leave"

As you saw in chapter 3, what sets highly happy couples apart more than anything else might be what starts out as a choice but ends up as a deep belief that their spouses have the best intentions toward them. And that includes believing that their spouses are not going to leave.

Carly began her marriage with intense love for her husband but, like many women, with a private insecurity about whether he felt the same way about her. She found herself worrying if he was *truly* in it forever. Look at how everything changed when she realized that he was:

There was a point in my marriage when things changed. It was somewhat early on, six years in, no kids yet. I was still insecure in my marriage. I was being the girl, you know, thinking, *There is no way he could love me as deeply as I love him. There's no way.*

Now, we don't fight—we just don't. We are both calm usually and sort through things—but this time we had an awful fight. All my insecurity came out. We were driving to meet some friends for dinner, and I'm crying, and he pulled the car over and said, "When are you going to get this—that I'm *in* this! I'm in this for the long haul. Quit being so insecure and *just believe.* Every time I say something cross with you doesn't mean that I'm going to leave. I'm still going to be here. We are not going to be a statistic."

Wow. For him, that was just a little point. But I'm telling you, hearing that from him struck a chord. From that point on, I took on a confidence in the marriage. He's *still* here. He *chose* me. Done. Our marriage isn't going to be a statistic.

Once he said that, I let go of insecurity and invested emotionally 100 percent in the fact that he's going to be here. And that is when our marriage turned around completely.

4. "We Work at It"

The happy couples are not just those who are determined to be married. As that wife who is now a premarital counselor put it earlier, the successful couples are those who are determined to have a *good* marriage.

And for many marriages, *determination* is indeed the right word. While some Yes! couples said it had been largely easy, most said they had to work at it—with some emphasizing that it had been hard at times. But the payoff for that effort is usually so sweet. Here's what one happy pastor's wife told me:

Something I've told women is that if you are married and you've decided that you are going to stay married, and he's your one and only—he is what you make him! You can be negative about him and complain and knock him down and beat him up, but you all are one. So your complaining and ungratefulness get you nowhere. But thanking God for him and praising him and finding the good in him and building him up ends up being for his good *and* your good *because you are one.* You just have to make a decision about that and stick to it.

For many, making that decision and sticking to it had included fighting for their marriages and getting help as needed along the way.

One very happy wife told me, "We both come from extremely broken homes. And because we had no guidance when we got married, I told him *we have to* take the marriage class at our church. We should have done premarital counseling, but since we didn't, we *are* going to take the marriage class after. And when we went into a tailspin later, we got counseling. We needed to know what it is to be married. We wanted foundations! It was awkward sometimes, but doing that stuff has made us what we are now."

Sometimes, you have to fight for marriage. Because it is worth fighting for!

Once You Commit, You'll Get
What You Want

For many people, the idea of complete, full, all-in commitment is a relief. For others, it can seem daunting and perhaps irrational. But as one Yes! husband put it,

> I honestly was a little worried about the commitment. It felt like I was jumping off a cliff. But what I found is that being intentional makes committing easy. You're taking one step at a time, so instead of the commitment being like jumping off the cliff, it's more like walking a staircase. And this is going to sound so sappy, but my personal experience has been that it's the stairway to heaven, so to speak. Once there is the actual commitment, and you're doing little things toward building commitment every day, it doesn't feel like as big of a step. [Looking at his wife] Every morning I get up, I choose to stay married to you.

And that choice means everything for happiness in marriage. If you feel that you might be holding back *in ways that are unhealthy,* think through how you might do things differently, pray about it, and talk to some friends or mentors who will give you good, biblical counsel (instead of just what you want to hear!). Then try some alternative ways of thinking and acting. Realize also that it may be a good heads-up for you to seek counseling or coaching about it at some point.

One might think that not protecting yourself and having no "just in case" plan would increase uncertainty and make you more insecure. Instead, everything I heard from the Yes! couples was the opposite. When there is no other option and you fully invest emotionally because you *have* to make it work, it dramatically *increases* commitment, certainty, and security. Taking the risk to be all in dramatically lowers uncertainty; taking the risk, in fact, lowers the risk!

> When there is no other option
> and you fully invest emotionally
> because you have to make it work,
> it dramatically increases commitment,
> certainty, and security.

As one man, fifteen years into a happy second marriage, put it, "Keeping my options open leads to anxiousness because I am worrying about the what-ifs or 'What am I missing?' I'm unsettled. There's an uncertainty, and that certainly leads to a lack of peace. Whereas if I'm all in, I'm committed; it makes it easy. There's peace because that's the only option. Knowing there's an eject seat will always contribute to dissatisfaction."

He continued, "There is a cultural shift today that says 'I won't commit until I get everything I want in another person.' But in real life, once you commit, you'll get what you want. Many people don't understand that commitment causes love. Causes passion. Today, I see it is a great thing."

Survey Says

Some spouses feel that since so many relationships encounter problems, it is important to maintain a bit of emotional independence or retain your own life in some way. That way, if everything falls apart, you still retain a piece of yourself. Is that true of you, or not true of you?

	Highly Happy Couples	Mostly Happy Couples	Struggling Couples
Yes, I do feel that way.	28%	38%	54%
No, I do not feel that way.	72%	62%	46%

Nationally representative and churchgoers' results combined.

13

Highly Happy Couples Think They Hit the Jackpot

Why Giving Credit Means Getting Back Bliss

C all it living in a state of wonder. Or call it the power of conscious gratitude. Whatever you call it, it is one of the sources of energy that turns a good marriage into a great one. Talk to consistently happy spouses for very long and you'll hear things like this bubbling out:

- "I can't believe he chose me."
- "I keep wondering when she's going to figure out that I'm not as amazing as she thinks I am."
- "How did I luck out like this?"

- "I'm convinced that if weren't for him, I would still be single."
- "Yeah, buddy, I sure outkicked my coverage."

Over and over, in the interviews with Yes! couples, I heard these casual remarks about something that really wasn't casual at all: a deeply felt gratitude. The feeling was much more fundamental than your everyday positive mental attitude. These folks lived in a state of awe that their spouses were in their lives—that they had chosen them in the first place!—and with the daily awareness that a huge part of their happiness was due to these wonderful people to whom they were joined.

Even when these couples were dealing with real problems—money, kids, sex, and a host of other things that can drain a marriage—each partner still *believed that they personally hit the jackpot.* I would state this powerful little secret like this:

💡 Highly happy spouses give their mate most of the credit for their relationship success—and they live in regular, conscious gratitude as a result.

As one happy husband put it, "I had no idea that marriage could be this good or how amazing she would be as a wife. I sure hit the jackpot with her. And I had no idea of the size of the jackpot when I pulled the lever."

When Giving the Credit Means
Living in Gratitude

In my personal opinion, this survey result is one of the most telling of them all: in nearly eight out of ten highly happy marriages, *each spouse gives the credit to their mate* for happiness in their marriage! (See graph.)

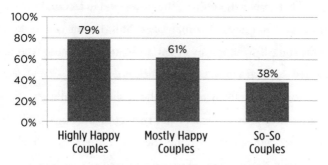

Percent of those who say their spouse is the reason their marriage is happy

Asked of those survey takers who responded in one of the first three categories of happiness ("Yes!" "Yes, mostly," or "Sometimes yes; sometimes no") when asked, "Are you generally happy in your marriage?" This question was not asked of those who answered "Not really" or "No!"

Not so with less than happy couples. By contrast, the majority of so-so couples indicate that *they* are the primary reason for a happy marriage; that they, personally, are the ones holding things together.

But perhaps you're doubtful. You might be thinking, *Well, maybe those who say they are responsible for the happiness of the marriage are empirically correct!*

> In nearly eight out of ten
> highly happy marriages, each
> spouse gives the credit to
> their mate!

That absolutely could be the case—and in fact undoubtedly *is* the case in quite a few marriages! Still, I want you to notice something: In the results of the so-so couples (those who answered "sometimes yes; sometimes no" on the survey), *each* spouse was more likely to believe he or she personally was doing more than the other person. But they both can't be correct. By contrast, *both* spouses among the Yes! couples were likely to give credit to the other person. And they can't both be correct either!

In other words, someone's happiness in their marriage (or lack thereof) may have far more to do with their *perception* of their spouse than with any empirically accurate list of their spouse's contributions or failures.

Do you see the gain for the spouses in a Yes! marriage? And

the hope for those who want one? Those who, as one woman put it, "allow themselves to really see the 'amazingness' of their spouses" and give them most of the credit improve their marriages via their own conscious gratitude!

When What You See Is What You Get

The Roman philosopher Cicero wrote, "Gratitude is not only the greatest of virtues, but the parent of all others." The marital experience of Yes! spouses seemed to bear this out. Their conscious gratitude for their mates seemed to have the effect of tempering other concerns and making them much happier in their marriages.

After all, with such an amazing person, *Does it really matter if he isn't that neat? Does it really matter that much if she always runs late?* Or, *Yes, this has been a bad year financially, but she is amazing the way she has stood beside me.* Or, *He has been so sweet the way he has reassured me we will get through this.*

And in being so aware of their partner's "amazingness" (I love that word!), these folks certainly did not take each other for granted nor overlook the great things that were right before their eyes. In the end, they expected fewer problems—and found fewer! Putting it another way, their perception *became* reality. What each saw in the other became what each experienced.

Interestingly, the power of perception is in line with what other researchers have found. Let's go back to Brad Wilcox at the University of Virginia. This is what he told me about how perception positively shapes reality in happy marriages:

> Shared housework was a predictor of happiness, for both husbands and wives, in our survey of those ages 18 to 46 with kids at home. But the reason *why* is what's interesting. For the average wife and husband, the perception in your head that you and your spouse are sharing housework and kids is what is linked to a happy marriage. If you run a clock on who is actually doing what, usually it will show that the wife does more. *But the perception that "it is shared" is what matters, even more than the actual time spent.*[16]

Now with that in mind, think about my survey finding that the happiest spouses give the credit to their mates, not to themselves. Since perception creates reality, it makes us much happier in our marriages when we truly believe that although we are both trying, our spouses are the ones who are *really* amazing—and their kindness or patience (or whatever) is what is most responsible for making us happy.

"I Totally Lucked Out!"

Sometimes at the end of the portion of our marriage conferences where we help men understand women, Jeff or I will read a quote from the end of our book *For Men Only*, as we illustrate how most wives feel about their husbands.

In this particular passage, an anonymous woman describes how grateful she is to be married to her husband. She relates a few things she really appreciates and then says, "The fact that I get to live with him over the course of my lifetime is one of the biggest scams I've pulled off."

> "The fact that I get to live with him over the course of my lifetime is one of the biggest scams I've pulled off."

Almost always, when we get to that quote, there is a roar from the crowd as men hear those words—and then are shocked to see the woman next to them nodding her head to say "Yep, that's how I feel too."

But here's the thing: whether happy, mostly happy, struggling, confused, delighted, rich, poor, black, white, old, young, first marriage or third—most spouses *feel* this gratitude on a regular basis. Yet it so often goes unsaid. Not so in highly happy marriages. In these relationships, *the spouses routinely make sure the other person knows that they feel that way*. One happy wife described it beautifully:

> My husband thinks that I think he is too uptight, overly involved in every home project, highly anxious, slightly moody, and has difficulty problem solving at times. I know he thinks that I am a little disorganized, too quick to jump to conclusions, not always communicative enough, and, let's face it, a bit of a slob. But you know what? We have *never* given the other person the impression that we have done anything but lucked out to find each other. That's the bottom line, and it smooths over a multitude of sins!

Clearly, for anyone who wants to have a highly happy marriage, cultivating gratitude for the other person—and letting them know how grateful you are—is vital.

But how do you do that?

> Clearly, for anyone who wants to have a highly happy marriage, cultivating gratitude for the other person—and letting them know how grateful you are—is vital.

How to Mind Your "Gratitudes"

In chapter 2, I mentioned the sudden, unexpected divorce of a couple who was close to us. The pain of witnessing the end of the marriage had become a catalyst for change in a wife in our mutual group of friends. She said she always had been grateful for her husband, although she admitted it was "a general thankfulness" that didn't get expressed often enough. But things were changing for her. She explained,

> Watching them fall apart has made me so much more attentive to focusing on the good and harping on the good, not on the bad. *Thank you for changing the light bulbs, and I'm not going to mention that you didn't take out the trash.* I'm trying to be purposeful now—about feeling it *and* saying it.

I like her example: be purposeful about feeling your gratitude, and be purposeful in saying it too. Her words remind me of the apostle Paul's admonition to the church in Thessalonica: "Be joyful always; pray continually; give thanks in all circumstances, for this is God's will for you in Christ Jesus."

Where you actually start in cultivating your "I hit the jackpot!" attitude is probably very close at hand. Over and over, the Yes! couples I talked to mentioned the simplest things:

- Name the specific things for which you are (or can be) grateful.
- Remember that even when times are difficult, there are *always* things about the other person to be thankful for.
- Each day, tell your spouse at least one thing you are grateful for about him or her. For example, "You're such a great mom to our kids; I love how much compassion you have when they are hurt, when I would tell them to suck it up and tough it out." Or, "I'm so grateful you aren't letting the layoff turn you into a grumpy dad. Thanks so much for modeling a good attitude to the kids during this time."
- Write your gratitudes down. That way they are explicit to you, and they'll come more quickly to mind and in conversation.

We don't have to wait until we lose what we love to realize its value. We can start today to change the weather in our marriages by intentionally minding our gratitudes—and letting our spouses know how blessed we feel because of them.

Survey Says

If you had to pick either you or your spouse as the primary reason why your marriage is happy and you enjoy being married, who would you pick?

	Highly Happy Couples	Mostly Happy Couples	So-So Couples
Me.	21%	39%	55%
My spouse.	79%	61%	38%
We are not that happy, so this doesn't apply to me.	0%	0%	7%

Asked of those survey-takers who responded in one of the first three categories of happiness ("Yes!" "Yes, mostly," or "Sometimes yes, sometimes no") when asked, "Are you generally happy in your marriage?"

This question was not asked of those who answered "Not really" or "No!"

14

Putting the Secrets to Work

Your Plan for Getting from So-So to Highly Happy in Your Marriage

As you have listened in on the lives and lessons of the happiest couples, have you wondered, *Can I really do this in my relationship?* And, *Does this stuff really make a difference?* I want to reassure you, you can, and it does. For all the research I've conducted over the years, I'm still the average nonpsychologist wife, and if I can put these secrets to work, you can too! The years that I've been researching these secrets of the Yes! couples have been some of the happiest in our marriage, in part because little by little, Jeff and I started applying these in our own relationship.

To get you started, I want to take you inside an important lesson I learned as I was wrapping up the main research for the book. I wanted see how couples of different ages, cultural backgrounds, and stages of life applied these habits in the real world—and to see whether they worked!—so I was thrilled when about ten different couples volunteered to test these habits over a six-week period. I gave them an overview of all the surprising secrets, and they excitedly got started.

And almost no one finished!

Huh?

When we dug into what had happened, we were relieved to discover that the secrets *did* work—just not when you try to learn them all at once! "It is difficult to keep all these things in our minds all the time," some folks told us. Or "We just have so much going on" or "I think we'll have to do this later." Trying to focus on everything at once was overwhelming, so it was easier to just not do any of it.

We learned an invaluable lesson with that first group about the importance of tackling these habits in bite-sized pieces. About starting small. About the beauty of remembering only one or two things at a time and not worrying about the rest for a while. Armed with those lessons and others, we recruited the next set of couples—and heard some amazing things.

When we asked the participants in our second experiment

group, "Are these tips making any difference for you, such as increasing your happiness or level of contentment in your marriage?" here is how one wife responded:

> Yes! They are tips I was not expecting to be the real key
> to happiness. I thought it would have to be something so
> secret, so difficult to achieve…but actually it is common
> sense, easy to put into place, and fun to find ways to apply
> it to our marriage!

So what is it, specifically, that makes the difference for those who end up being able to apply these secrets of happy couples in a practical, life-changing way? Like the Yes! couples themselves, what are these men and women doing differently—and what can you and your mate do too? Here are ten tips.

Ten Anyone-Can-Do-Them Tips

1. Identify What You Are Already Doing Well

Either on your own or (ideally) with your spouse, go through the list of habits in this book and identify what you are already doing well. Give yourself credit! Seeing the things you already do (perhaps without realizing it) is key to keeping them going for the long run.

2. Pick Your Bite: Choose One or Two
Habits—Max—to Try at a Time

To make big changes, start small. Don't be like the test group that got so excited about the habits that they tried to do all of them, and thus didn't end up doing any of them. Pick *only one or two habits to practice,* ideally for several weeks. And even narrow it down to one particular habit within a habit where necessary!

If you're feeling confident, another option that a lot of couples liked is for each spouse to pick a habit (or sub-habit) for the other, and for you both to pick one to try together.

3. Be Ready to Connect the Dots

Don't wait for the perfect time, because—news flash—there probably *won't* be any perfect time! So start now, and be ready to watch and connect a given effort with a given result, from day one. Some habits build happiness over time, but others (such as the little things covered in chapter 2) may make a difference almost immediately.

As one woman told me rather sheepishly, "What this test did for me was allow me to connect the dots. I wasn't that surprised that my husband picked starting with the little things. And since I already say thank you a lot, for him I knew the issue was really his desire to have sex more than a couple of times a month. But what I wouldn't have noticed before was just how big of an emotional difference that made to him. He was so much sweeter and gentler the next day. Suddenly I really *saw* that it matters much more to him and to us than I realized."

4. Try These Habits Alone If You Have to—It Still Works!

Even if one spouse is reluctant, you can still start. Each habit requires just *one* partner to begin, and all of them *will help to make you both happy, even if just one of you does them.* The Yes! couples aren't just doing these things because they are already happy—they are happy because they are doing these things. Quite a few of the happiest couples I spoke with started out in the struggling category and changed *because* just one partner began implementing these habits.

Although there will always be a few sad cases where someone doesn't reciprocate, the amazing paradox of following God's command to "look not only to your own interests, but also to the interests of others"—in other words, showing that you care about what matters to the other person—will often result in the other person's *wanting* to do the same.

During the experiment, one husband in a struggling marriage, who was working on trying to believe the best, submitted this anonymous note:

I still find it very hard to believe that there is no intent to guilt or shame when she says some of the things she does. But I'm trying! There were a couple of times when I wanted very much to remind her of the principles *she* was supposed to be following during this period, but I had to hold myself back. And I'm glad I did, because I see us much softer toward each other than we were just a few weeks ago.

5. Plug Into Community

So many couples said that it was much easier to apply these things when they were talking with other couples and touching base regularly—for example, once a week in a small group—instead of trying to practice them solely on their own. For the person making changes solo in a marriage, the support of others is especially important. Enlist at least one other couple to work along with you to implement these habits.

6. Listen to and Lean on God

Pray for God's guidance before you make the final choice of what to start with—or what your spouse should start with! As one husband cautioned, "For example, there might be one thing that you think your husband just needs to do. You may be absolutely sure! But when you pray about it, God might say, *No, this other thing is what I want you to ask him to do…because he* can do *this one, and that will then give him confidence to try others.* Giving this process to God and asking for His guidance is so key."

And then while you're putting these insights to work, pray with and for each other, and then connect *those* dots to see what your heavenly Father does as a result.

7. Create Reminders

Nearly every participant mentioned something about the importance of reminding yourself to keep what you're working on front and center. Otherwise, as one put it, "The busyness of life will probably distract you from thinking about it. My wife had me working on pulling myself out of a funk since I was in a really bad mood about my job. And every night I would see this sticky note I wrote myself asking, 'Are you grumpy?' And it was a shocker at first how often I answered yes! It made me think. I worked at it, simply because I was conscious of it for the first time."

8. Stick with It

All these habits are based on choice, not feelings (at least at first!). Make a commitment to do what you can do and stick with it.

Give each one a try for some predetermined number of weeks before moving on to the next. Let it sink in. Maybe journal the results. But be aware every day that you are building a habit, and that requires consistent *action*. Even if, on some of these, the only action is that you purposefully change your thoughts!

A husband in one of our test groups emphasized, "I found I have to make a daily effort to practice what I chose to try... It is an act of the will."

9. Be Generous with Yourself and Each Other

This is a marathon, not a sprint. This is a new lifestyle of learning. If you stumble, that's okay. Get up and take another step instead of letting it totally stop you. When I asked the experimenting couples what we could do to help people apply these habits well, one wife answered,

> We got in a disagreement early in the experiment, and
> that thwarted our progress. It would be so good if you
> could preface the whole thing by saying, "You know,
> arguments might happen, problems might happen, and
> that's okay. At least you are trying to make your marriage
> better. Don't let it stop you from really doing this."

And if your spouse stumbles, that's okay too. As one man told me, "It is so important to focus on staying positive and focused on the long term. Because you really don't know what your spouse's starting point was, internally. They may be making tremendous strides inside, given where they are starting from. Don't look at the short-term stuff. It may not paint the best picture of the real change that is happening underneath."

10. Celebrate Results!

As you see results, celebrate them! Talk with your wife about how great it feels now that she's saying "Thank you." Applaud your husband for how loved his new approach has made you feel. Ideally, even if you aren't the journaling type, write things down and capture what changed so you can encourage yourself later when it is needed.

For example, think about how encouraging it would be for this particular wife to look back on the note she wrote about her first habit ("Believe the Best"): "I feel like this has improved my outlook, and I do appreciate the fact that most of the time, my husband does have my best interest at heart. I don't know why I would ever think otherwise, but I feel that over this time period, I believe it!"

A Lifestyle of Learning...Together

Several couples compared these new habits to a lifestyle change—a new lifestyle of learning that leads to so much more enjoyment every day. When we asked the test couples "What did you like best about participating in this experiment?" one husband submitted this:

> I enjoyed that it prompted my wife and me to not be
> complacent. Even though I would say we have a terrific
> marriage, it does require constant tending. It showed me
> that no matter how great our marriage is, there is always
> room to grow. There is always more to learn. But that just
> makes it even better.

Years ago, when we were graduate students and not yet engaged, Jeff asked our pastor if he could get some advice about our relationship. Walden Pond wasn't that far away, so the two of them walked the trails around the pond for a few hours. Our pastor knew that Jeff had been praying about our relationship for some time. But Jeff was also questioning whether the wisest course was to take things slow—whether he and I should both move to the same city after graduation and wait another year or two to get engaged.

Our pastor looked thoughtful. "What would be your reason for waiting?"

"Well…we've been friends for less than a year. I was thinking we should take another year or two so we can get to know each other even better. There are still things I don't know about her."

Our pastor chuckled. "I've been married to Elizabeth for seventeen years. And every day I learn something new about her. As you grow and mature, everyone changes; there are always new things to uncover. There will never come a moment when you know everything there is to know. But continuing to learn each other is part of the fun of marriage. The key is to trust God, make a decision…and start."

As we look to the future, those words can be a great encouragement to each of us.

Let's be ready to continue to learn about each other and have fun doing it. To watch in hope for big, happy changes to come from these small, simple steps. To trust God for the outcome. And start.

Acknowledgments

For a book and research study that required skilled expertise, input, analysis, investigation, insight, support, and referrals from many dozens of people over the course of three years, I am profoundly aware that a short acknowledgments section will never give me the space to thank the many people without whom this book wouldn't exist. Although I can list only a fraction here, please know that I am immensely grateful for the contribution made by every single person who has touched this book.

To Linda Crews, my tremendous staff director, and Cathy Kidd, Jenny Reynolds, Theresa Colquitt, Karen Newby, Sally van der Riet, Tally Whitehead, Kathy Dunmon, Debbie Licona, Melinda Weedon, and Naomi Duncan—my past and current staff team and researchers who worked on this book and who are working today to keep everything moving forward so I can focus on writing and speaking: You all are amazing. Just *amazing*. I am grateful every single day for you. Cathy and Jenny, I am particularly grateful for your excellent in-depth work during the research and investigation process, which shaped the whole book. Tally, I'm so blessed to have partnered with you in marriage research for so many years, most especially on *The Good News About Marriage* findings that have been so important for this book as well.

To Calvin Edwards, my amazing literary agent, consultant, and friend: the content of every one of my research studies and all these books has been built from the ground up by your insight and help. Jeff and I are so grateful for our friendship with you and Nerida. I'll forever be grateful for our miraculous meeting fifteen years ago.

To Chuck Cowan and the team at Analytic Focus (www.analyticfocus.com), especially Mauricio Vidaurre and Mauricio Semino: Thank you, again, for the unwavering excellence, support, time, and interest you bring to these research projects. Chuck, your partnership means a lot and has been a major, major part of why these books have impacted millions of readers over the years. Thank you.

To Felicia Rogers, Ramiro Davila, and the wonderful crew at Decision Analyst (www.decisionanalyst.com): Each time we work together, I am so grateful for such excellent and enthusiastic people. I appreciate you all.

To the tremendous researchers who have studied marriage for years and who have allowed me to partner with them to look at their data in a new way—most important, Brad Wilcox and Sam Sturgeon with the National Marriage Project, and Clint Jenkin and Pam Jacob at the Barna Group: I'm honored by your willingness to provide insight, data, and support for these projects. And I am deeply grateful for the leadership you offer in these fields. I am also so thankful to the many coaches, counselors, pastors, psychologists, and other leaders who have shared their hard-won experience.

This book would never have happened without hundreds of personal interviews with happy couples, and dozens of those interviews came via the referrals and time-intensive help from some extraordinarily generous friends and strangers around the country, especially Bruce and Sue Osterink, Allan and Tricia Beeber, Charles and Rebecca Gilmer, and many, many others, including the team at Family Life who allowed me to conduct a major survey on a marriage cruise. I'm also blown away by the help of several sponsors of marriage events, who allowed us to conduct surveys as part of our time together. Most important, I am so grateful for the hundreds of married couples who either sat for scheduled interviews or allowed me to randomly interrupt them at coffee shops, on airplanes, and everywhere in between, and ask questions. Although all interviewees are anonymous, you know who you are, and I'm very grateful for your generosity and honesty.

A special thank-you to the team at Perimeter Church and the Marriage Hour, especially Kipper Tab, Mac and Barbara Kaiser, and Joe and Judy Tjoe: You all have surrounded us, helped us in so many ways, allowed us to experiment on you...and become our new family. Thank you.

To the wonderful team at WaterBrook Multnomah, especially my amazing editors, Dave Kopp, Susan Tjaden, Amy McDonell, Laura Wright, and Helen MacDonald, as well as Steve Cobb, Ken Petersen, Carie Freimuth, Allison O'Hara, Lori Addicott and the rest of the family: I continue to be so humbled and grateful every day for my partnership with you. You go far above and beyond in supporting and encouraging me, even including setting up focus groups for this book! (Thank you, Renee Nyen!)

To my prayer team: You do the real work. Thank you for praying for me, for your commitment, and for your faithfulness even when I forget to ask. To our special friends and prayer partners, Lisa and Eric Rice and the "anti home group" home group gang, Darlene and Ken Penner, Scott and Patti Benjamin, and Jeff and Jen Cole: our lives are forever changed because of you.

To my kids: Dear ones, you are delightful. I love you so, so much. Thank you for your patience when I have to be locked in my office, for your hugs when I'm tired, for your prayers when I'm discouraged, and for your constant, constant love. Dad and I are in awe of the godly young woman and godly young man that you are becoming.

To my husband: Bud, I could do none of this without you. Your support is constant and unwavering. Your encouragement and strength hold me up when I don't know how I can keep going. Your patience gives me a standard to aim for. Your insight has impacted every word of every book…indeed, everything I do. And your love makes me want to be a better wife and a better person, every day. I love my life. And every single day I am grateful to the One who created marriage and brought us together.

Notes

1. Earlier research had shown me that the relationship lessons from men and women in committed marriages were the most widely applicable to all other types of dating and partnered couples, whereas findings from those other couples were often more specialized and might or might not apply to married men and women. Also, because so much of this research was opposite-gender related, the surveys for this book, unlike some others, only included heterosexual men and women.

2. Since so much of my research deals specifically with the gaps in knowledge between the genders, this survey included only heterosexual individuals.

3. The great book *The Five Love Languages: The Secret to Love That Lasts* by Dr. Gary Chapman (Chicago: Northfield, 2010) helps readers identify what love language speaks most to their mates—for example, some people feel most loved when their spouses say something like "Sit down and rest while I do some of these chores," indicating that their love language is acts of service. What I found in this research complements (rather than contradicts) Dr. Chapman's

findings, but it also indicates that a few of the same specific things tend to matter to each gender *regardless* of what their actual love language is.

4. J. K. Rowling, *Harry Potter and the Order of the Phoenix* (New York: Scholastic, 2003), 516.

5. Kurt Gray, "The Power of Good Intentions: Perceived Benevolence Soothes Pain, Increases Pleasure, and Improves Taste," *Social Psychological and Personality Science* 3, no. 5 (2012): 639–45.

6. Dr. Brad Wilcox (director of the National Marriage Project at the University of Virginia), in an interview with the author, Charlottesville, Virginia, December 27, 2011.

7. Dr. Brad Wilcox, *Survey of Marital Generosity, 2010–2011.* Special data run from Dr. Wilcox to cross-tabulate by marital happiness categories, August 28, 2013. The survey was conducted with married men and women ages 18 to 55, who had children. The logistic regression model also adjusted for participants' age, education, household income, and race/ethnicity. Although couples were grouped in similar categories to mine, since this was a different survey conducted in a different way, I have titled the happy categories "very happy" and "happy" to distinguish the results from my own categories of "highly happy" and "mostly happy."

8. Wilcox, *Survey of Marital Generosity*. *Above-average generosity* was defined as having a score on the generosity scale that was higher than the mean.

9. Wilcox, *Survey of Marital Generosity*. *Above-average quality time* was defined as a score of 4 or higher (on a scale of 1 to 6) on a question that asked participants, "During the past month, about how often did you and your husband/wife spend time alone with each other, talking or sharing an activity?"

10. This quote and variations of it have also been attributed to Plato and to the nineteenth-century Scottish author Ian Maclaren.

11. As noted in chapter 1, whenever I address issues of faith in this book, I'm primarily talking about Christian beliefs. Although my analysis and surveys (and that of others) certainly included those of many other religious beliefs (Jewish, Muslim, and so on), there simply weren't large enough sample sizes to draw definitive conclusions.

12. See my upcoming book *The Good News About Marriage* (Colorado Springs: Multnomah, 2014).

13. Feldhahn, *Good News*.

14. Leonce Crump, pastor of Renovation Church, preaching in the Atlanta area on February 5, 2012. He was speaking on racial reconciliation, but it struck me that his comment was

also a perfect summary of what I heard from so many Yes! couples about marriage.

15. See *The Good News About Marriage* for the details of all numbers mentioned here about the divorce rate, rate of happiness, and so on.

16. Wilcox, interview with the author, December 27, 2011, emphasis added.